BEAD
Sparkle

120 DESIGNS
FOR EARRINGS, NECKLACES, BRACELETS & MORE

SUSAN BEAL

To Pearl & Everett, who add the sparkle

The Taunton Press
Inspiration for hands-on living®

The Taunton Press, Inc.
63 South Main Street, PO Box 5506
Newtown, CT 06470-5506
e-mail: tp@taunton.com

Editors: Ashley Little, Shawna Mullen, Tim Stobierski
Copy editor: Betty Christiansen
Indexer: Barbara Mortenson
Interior and cover design and layout: Kathie Alexander
Illustrator: Alexis Hartman
Photographer: Tom Moore
Stylist: Karen Donohue

The following names/manufacturers appearing in *Bead Sparkle* are trademarks: Aleene's® Jewel-It Embellishing Glue™, Aleene's® Original Tacky Glue®, Aleene's® Platinum Bond 7800®, Bakelite®, Beacon 527®, Dremel®, E6000®, Fabri-Tac™, Fray Check™, JoAnn Fabric and Craft Stores®, JudiKins Diamond Glaze™, Lacy's Stiff Stuff™, Lucite®, Michaels®, Mod Podge®, Nymo®, Phoomph™, Soft Flex®, Thread Heaven Thread Conditioner and Protectant®

Library of Congress Cataloging-in-Publication Data

Names: Beal, Susan, author.
Title: Bead sparkle : 120 designs for earrings, necklaces, bracelets & more / Susan Beal.
Description: Newtown, CT : Taunton Press, Inc., [2016] | Includes index.
Identifiers: LCCN 2016007224 | ISBN 9781631861543
Subjects: LCSH: Jewelry making.
Classification: LCC TT212 .B427 2016 | DDC 745.594/2--dc23
LC record available at https://lccn.loc.gov/2016007224

Printed in the United States of America
10 9 8 7 6 5 4 3 2 1

ACKNOWLEDGMENTS

I've heard that writing a book is a little like climbing a mountain—and I guess there are plenty of parallels, since you just put one foot in front of the other and keep going (or keep designing more and more pieces of jewelry, noting everything in spreadsheets as you go!). Thank you so much to everyone who made this particular mountain a little easier to conquer, and a lot more fun.

Thanks so much to my wonderful guest contributors, whose gorgeous projects were a huge inspiration—Christina Batch-Lee, Michelle Freedman, Lynzee Malsin, Torie Nguyen, Kayte Terry, and Cathy Zwicker. I'm lucky to have you as friends and collaborators! Thanks to my editor, Shawna Mullen, who invited me to create an eight-years-later sequel to *Bead Simple*, and to Timothy Stobierski, whose thoughtful focus at every step of the manuscript and book process really brought this new project to life. Ashley Little's creative eye and editor's mind were each equally helpful, Carolyn Mandarano oversaw everything beautifully, and Betty Christiansen's copy edits brought clarity and consistency. Thanks to photographer Tom Moore and his stylist Karen Donohue for the lush, colorful images, and to my longtime illustrator, Alexis Hartman, for contributing the elegant illustrations and diagrams she always does so well.

My agent, Stacey Glick, is a tireless advocate, from the very first draft of a proposal to the final cover review, and I can't thank her enough for her support. I also appreciate the wonderful people and shops who make and sell the beautiful pieces that inspired so many of my new jewelry designs: special thanks to a few of my Portland favorites, Maria at Collage, Lynzee at Dava Bead, and Mary, Tawnya, and Stacy at the Pendleton Woolen Mill Store.

My kids, Pearl and Everett, generously share their love of color, sparkle, and shape, always telling me which pieces they like and which ones they absolutely love. And finally, after seventeen years together (and eight books), you get to know someone pretty well; my husband, Andrew, is a superstar, always cheering me on and keeping me going. Thank you, for everything.

Contents

Introduction 2

1. Getting Started 4
Tools 5
Materials 6
Beads 10
Mixed Media and Ephemera 12
Vintage Treasures 13
Stringing 14
Needles 14
Cords, Wires, and Threads 14
Design 16
Color 16

2. Techniques 18
Bead Stringing 19
Wirework 23
Knotting 30
Stitching 30
Jewelry Repair 33

THE PROJECTS 34

3. Earrings 36
Pop of Color Earrings 37
Just a Little Sparkle Earrings 41
Nature-Inspired Earrings 45
Geometric Earrings 48
Semiprecious Earrings 52
My Favorite Earrings 55
Vintage Gone Modern Earrings 59

4. Necklaces 61
Geometric Necklaces 62
Nature-Inspired Necklaces 65
Semiprecious Necklaces 69
Holiday Party Necklaces 72
Tiered Necklaces 77
Statement Necklaces 82
My Favorite Necklaces 85
Vintage Gone Modern Necklaces 89

5. Pendants 93

Family Pendants 94
Lucky Charm Pendants 98
Semiprecious Pendants 101
Nature-Inspired Pendants 105
Geometric Pendants 109
My Favorite Pendants 112
Vintage Gone Modern Pendants 116

6. Brooches & Barrettes 119

Nature-Inspired Brooches & Barrettes 120
Embellished Hair Combs 124
Geometric Brooches & Barrettes 128
Semiprecious Brooches & Barrettes 131
My Favorite Brooches & Barrettes 135
Vintage Gone Modern Brooches &
    Barrettes 138

7. Bracelets 140

Charm Bracelet Deluxe 141
Nature-Inspired Bracelets 145
Semiprecious Bracelets 148
Geometric Bracelets 151
My Favorite Bracelets 155
Vintage Gone Modern
    Bracelets 158

8. Embellishments 161

Botanical Décor 162
Pretty Jars 165
Holiday Sparkle 168
Little Gifts 172
My Favorite Embellishments 175
Vintage Gone Modern
    Embellishments 178

Metric Equivalents 182
Guest Designers 183
Resources 184
Index 185

INTRODUCTION

Eight years ago, I wrote my first book, *Bead Simple*, and poured everything I knew about making jewelry and accessories into it, from delicate wirework to bold and graphic beading, and everything in between. I tried to make it as diverse and inclusive as possible, including super-simple beginner projects and gorgeously complicated advanced pieces alike.

The book took on a life of its own, through five printings and four spin-off booklets, and every time I saw it in a bookstore or a craft store, or heard from someone that they loved it, it made me so happy. Almost a decade later, after I'd written about sewing, quilting, making terrariums, buttons, and embroidery, the chance to write a new jewelry book came around . . . a sequel to my first one from so long ago, this time focusing on the extra-special pieces that add sparkle to your life.

At first I was a little overwhelmed—what could I possibly come up with after the first 150 projects I'd already shared? But given that wonderful chance, it was so much fun to create 120 new designs incorporating fresh directions, like cross-stitch, botanicals, painting, collage, and glass, as well as all the old favorite techniques like beading, wirework, and

knotting. The beautiful beads, buttons, and mixed-media materials I found sparked tons of new ideas, and in just a few months I'd finished the ten dozen projects, from a lucky pendant I wear almost every day now to a family birthstone earrings and locket set I save for very special occasions.

I updated and revised all my favorite parts of *Bead Simple*—the elegant illustrations and diagrams and clear techniques, the encouragement to create pieces in your own style spinning off from an inspiring central idea, and mixing vintage, new, found, and unexpected treasures to create your very own unique jewelry. I added ten new design principles, from careful use of negative space and mixing high and low to incorporating texture in your work. I'll always particularly love the vintage gone modern aesthetic, so I expanded it to a colorful

stand-alone section of every chapter, as you'll see when you flip through the book. And there are so many dazzling new jewelry and craft materials available now, so I got the chance to create lots of new pieces I couldn't have dreamed up eight years ago.

Whether you're new to jewelry-making or just looking for fresh inspiration, I hope this book brings you joy as you create. There's nothing quite like the instant pick-me-up of adding something sparkly to your life, whether it's a quick accessory choice to brighten up a Tuesday morning headed to work, or making something special for a New Year's Eve party to wear with a pretty new dress.

I'll borrow back what I wrote to introduce *Bead Simple*: Here's to making jewelry that makes you feel gorgeous!

—*Susan*

Tools, Materials, and Design Basics

Here's everything you'll need to get started designing your own gorgeous jewelry—basic tools, materials, and techniques.

TOOLS

A set of three **jewelry pliers** are essential for making your own pieces with wire:

Flat-nose pliers (also called chain-nose pliers) are perfect for flattening or forming sharp angles.

Round-nose pliers form smooth loops and curves. They are graduated in size, so you can form tiny loops around the narrow tips or larger ones farther back on the jaws.

Wire cutters are great for neatly clipping wires and cords.

Other pliers that are useful to have are **flattening pliers**, which have flat, plastic-lined jaws for wire straightening, and **hole-punch pliers**, which are perfect for making a small, precise hole through metal.

You can buy inexpensive pliers starting at about $6 each, which often come in a set, or higher-quality German-made pliers for about $20 each. The more expensive pliers have springs in the handles, which make them both easier to use and much more durable. You can always buy inexpensive tools first and upgrade to better-quality pieces when you are more experienced.

It's always nice to have sharp **scissors** on hand for cutting nonwire materials. For knotting, you can use long, skinny-tipped **tweezers** to grip the cord right where you want your knot to go.

You'll also use **glue** in some projects, especially to reinforce or embellish. Cement glue (recommended brand: Beacon 527®) is perfect for anchoring small findings, like a tip at the end of a piece of memory wire. Craft glue (recommended brand: Aleene's® Original Tacky Glue®) is ideal for attaching small, lightweight pieces to flat surfaces and will not damage the color or backing of a rhinestone. Special paper glue

Basic Tools

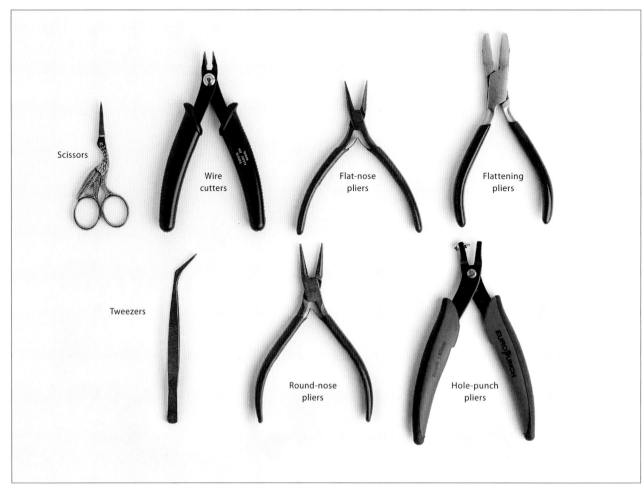

Scissors

Wire cutters

Flat-nose pliers

Flattening pliers

Tweezers

Round-nose pliers

Hole-punch pliers

(recommended brand: JudiKins Diamond Glaze™) is wonderful for joining paper to glass and dries clear and strong. A hot-glue gun often works well for joining larger or varied pieces to a base or to each other, and industrial-strength strong glue (recommended brand: E6000®) is the strongest bond of all, but make sure you use plenty of ventilation when you're gluing with it.

MATERIALS

Here are some of the materials that are most useful for beading and making your own jewelry. You can find most of them fairly inexpensively, and you can build up a collection as you go. Keep your work materials neatly organized in a fishing tackle box, small shelves or drawers, or plastic bins and bead boxes with snap-tight lids.

Findings

■ **Jump rings** are useful for joining two pieces together, like chains to clasps. A jump ring is just a circle of wire that isn't sealed shut—it can be opened with

pliers and then closed again. They come in a range of sizes, from about 3 mm (a small ring that's great for attaching a clasp to a thin chain) to 10 mm (a sizable ring for joining large pieces) and larger. In general, 22-gauge rings are useful for most projects.

■ **Soldered rings** are solid, with no openings. They're ideal for using with clasps and are available in the same sizes as jump rings.

■ **Split rings** are like key rings—you open one side and slip the ring onto a loop or chain. They're more secure than jump rings but harder to put on.

Findings

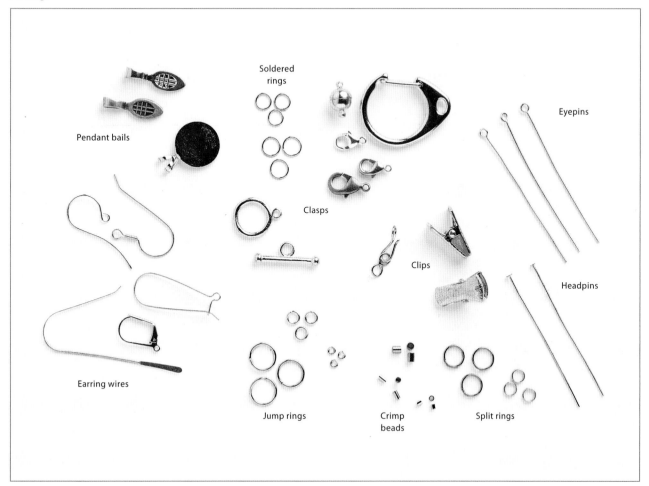

Pendant bails

Soldered rings

Eyepins

Clasps

Clips

Headpins

Earring wires

Jump rings

Crimp beads

Split rings

■ **Headpins,** which are straight pieces of wire with a stopper at one end, are perfect for making earrings, pendants, and other dangles.

■ **Eyepins** have a small loop at the end to serve as the stopper instead of a flat "head," so you can use a jump ring or another loop to join a dangle to your piece. You can easily make your own eyepins, too (see p. 28).

■ **Pendant bails** are just the thing for turning a flat-backed piece into a pretty pendant, and **pinbacks** make wonderful brooches.

■ **Earring wires** are sold commercially in dozens of styles, from simple drops and hooks to more elaborate leverbacks. Like wire, they're available in gold-filled, sterling silver, and base metal, plus other materials like surgical steel and niobium.

■ **Clasps** come in many forms, too, from plain to ornate—S-shapes, lobster claws, barrels, and toggles, to name just a few. (You'll learn how to make your own earring wires and clasps on p. 28.) One clasp that's great to use (especially for bracelets) is a magnetic style—so easy to open and close.

■ **Clips** of different types are useful for creating everything from sweater clips to fascinators, and **hair combs** (p. 8) embellish beautifully.

■ **Bracelet blanks and bangles** come in a nice range of styles and sizes (as shown on p. 8).

■ **Barrettes, bobby pins, and hair clips** (p. 8) are also a lot of fun to work with—they are perfect little canvases to build a design on.

Findings

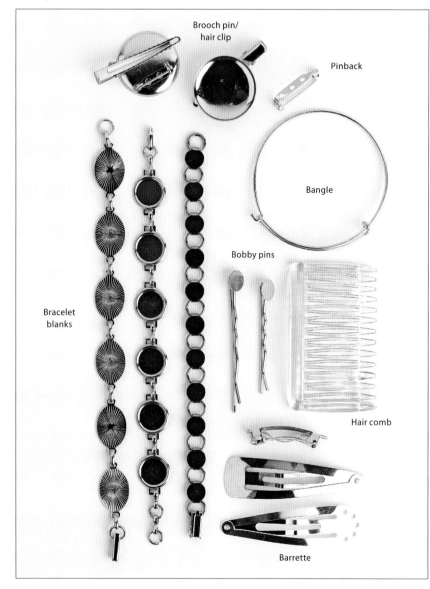

Brooch pin/
hair clip

Pinback

Bangle

Bobby pins

Bracelet
blanks

Hair comb

Barrette

Wire

Wire comes in different gauges, or thicknesses. The higher the gauge number, the thinner the wire. For many projects, **20-gauge** and **24-gauge wire** are perfect. The 20-gauge wire is thick enough to make earring wires, and the 24 is thin enough to use with small beads but is still durable. Heavier gauges like 16 are ideal for doing structural pieces, while more delicate gauges like 28 to 32 are so thin that they're almost like thread.

■ **Craft wire** is inexpensive and perfect for beginners to practice with. It comes in a variety of colors—metallics like silver, gold, and copper, as well as a rainbow of hues. Craft wire is generally a bit softer and more pliable than precious-metal wires; it's made of base metal, which is an alloy, or mixture, of different materials. Two things to keep in mind are that some people are sensitive to the nickel in base metal and may do better with sterling, and that the dull gray layer underneath the shiny surface may eventually show through over time.

■ **Sterling silver wire** is wonderful to work with. It comes in different hardnesses—I like **half-hard wire**, which has more strength and body than **dead soft**. Every sterling piece is marked 0.925, which means that it is at least 92.5 percent pure silver, with a few other metals to strengthen it. **Fine silver** is 100 percent pure, but it is softer and not suitable for some wirework projects.

■ **Gold-filled wire** combines pure gold with a base metal (typically 12K or 14K), since pure gold is very soft. It usually doesn't cause the kind of allergic reactions that base metals can trigger. Both gold and silver fluctuate in price, so the cost of wire often changes with the

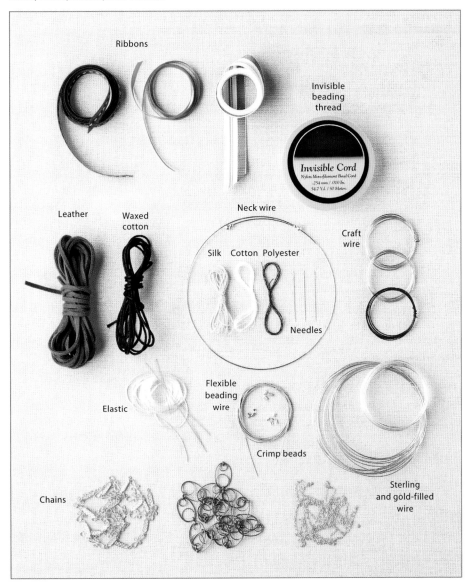

Ribbons

Invisible beading thread

Invisible Cord
Nylon Monofilament Bead Cord
.254 mm / .010 In.
54.7 Yd. / 50 Meters

Leather

Waxed cotton

Neck wire

Craft wire

Silk Cotton Polyester

Needles

Flexible beading wire

Elastic

Crimp beads

Chains

Sterling and gold-filled wire

market, but sterling silver is more afford-able than gold.

■ **Chain** comes in all sizes and weights, from delicate and lacy to thick and sturdy. When you buy it in bulk (by the foot or on a spool, for example), it's con-siderably cheaper than buying finished chains, and it's a breeze to put the clasps and finishers on yourself for a necklace that's exactly the length and style you want. You can also make a chain by joining jump rings in a continuous strand. (See "Jump rings" on p. 27 for more infor-mation on chain making.)

Wire gauges

16: heavy clasps or connectors

18: heavy clasps, sturdy jump rings

20: jump rings, plain loops, wrapped loops, stud-earring posts, heavy earring wires

22: earring wires, basic wire wrapping

24: earring wires, basic wire wrapping (wrapped loops), looping

26: delicate wirework (wrapped loops), lightweight loops

28 and above: delicate wrapping and loops, threading

BEADS

You can buy beads in every shape, size, color, and material, and in every price range, too, at local bead stores and shops online. You can also look for costume jewelry pieces at yard sales or thrift stores—take them apart and use the vintage beads to make your own unique designs. Buttons and rhinestones are fun to mix in, too.

Bead sizes are usually measured in millimeters. A 3-mm bead is tiny, an 8-mm bead is about the size of a pea, a 12-mm or 14-mm bead is on the small side of marble size, and so on. (See the chart on p. 12.)

■ **Seed beads** are tiny, typically solid-colored glass beads that are useful for creating space between bigger beads or stopping a larger piece from slipping over a thin headpin or small loop. They come in different sizes as well—as with wire-gauge measurements, the larger the number, the smaller the bead size. Use 11/0s for delicate projects, 8/0s for medium-size pieces, and 6/0s for crafting or embellishing. **Delicas** are high-quality seed beads with a precise, consistent size, while the less expensive versions have some differences in size and shape.

■ **Glass beads** come in all colors, sizes, and shapes. Look for smooth or faceted beads to add sparkle and shine in your designs. Glass is relatively heavy, so don't use larger pieces for earrings or string them on delicate material for necklaces or bracelets.

■ **Metal beads** and charms can range from tiny spacers to larger round and other shapes (which are often hollow), as well as gorgeous decorative drops

and decorations. They can have a tarnished, antiqued patina or a super-shiny finish. Metal beads and charms look great mixed with other materials—they add a lovely contrast and gleam to bright or dark colors. Like other findings, they are available in sterling and gold/gold-filled as well as base metals (copper, brass, and silver colors).

■ **Acrylic/plastic/Lucite® beads**, charms, molded pieces, and other components are beautiful and light-weight—perfect for adding tons of pop without a lot of weight. Look for vintage pieces in smooth or faceted finishes, or new ones in variegated colors or solids—there are so many styles of this versatile material.

■ **Wood beads** and drops range in size, shape, and color but give a natural, stylish look within a design. Since wood typically isn't especially heavy, you can use larger pieces within a necklace or pendant without adding a lot of weight.

■ **Semiprecious beads** are wonderful to work with, and there are dozens of stones to choose from. Some of my favorites are agates (like carnelian or smoky gray agate), which have a beautiful glossy tone; jades and aventurines in milky whites and greens; deep, dramatic dark-red garnets; citrines in serene warm tones; turquoise in blues, greens, or acid yellows; and pearls, ranging from smooth rounds to long, jagged points. Look for rounds, ovals, briolettes, cylinders, chunky abstract shapes, and tiny beads. Buying semiprecious beads on strands is usually the most economical way to go, but if

you buy individual beads, you can pick and choose exactly. Semiprecious beads are typically heavy, so use them sparingly as earrings and on thinner chains. One last note: Don't be afraid to use imitation stones! They can be as beautiful as the real thing and are often more ethical, more affordable, and just more fun.

■ **Buttons** are really wonderful for making jewelry or for embellishing. I love inexpensive casein, Bakelite®, or plastic buttons to design around—the colors, feel, and lightness are all very compelling. Covered buttons are a super-customized option to spotlight your favorite fabric prints. They come in a range of sizes and are very easy to put together for just the right finishing touch.

■ **Sequins** are beautiful extras to mix into a piece, whether you stitch or glue them down. Look for new or vintage sequins in interesting shapes or bright colors, and have fun with their layout and placement, mixing them with beads and rhinestones if you'd like.

■ **Rhinestones** are one of those perfect little elements that bring jewelry or accessories just the right dose of sparkle.

I use tiny ones as centers for sequins or flower cabs, or let larger ones tell a story as the main elements of a design. Some rhinestones are drilled so you can stitch them, and any with flat backs are easy to glue onto fabric, metal, or any other sturdy surface.

MIXED MEDIA AND EPHEMERA

I absolutely love to use craft supplies and ephemera in jewelry design. You'll see some of these materials in every chapter throughout the book, but some of my favorites are washi tape, a colorful and fun Japanese adhesive tape that offers a graphic pop; beautiful vintage postage stamps or other patterned bits; paper labels, flowers, or other shaped pieces; glass squares or rectangles, which show off any paper or washi with an interesting framing effect; fabric, which is wonderful for making covered buttons, bows, flowers, or backgrounds, or for adding texture; lace and appliqués, which can be an elegant base for designing around and on; silk floral, botanical, and leaf sprays, which are remarkably versatile and beautiful to work with; and interesting plastic or wooden shapes, like the star I found to create a little shadow box ornament (see p. 171).

Fabrics and threads

I love fabric, and sewing and quilting are a huge inspiration for my jewelry as well. Whether you're using pieces of your favorite print fabrics for making custom covered buttons, hand stitching, layering, or embellishing, the beautiful texture and color that textiles provide is unmatched. Pearl cotton in beautiful hues adds a special quality to simple cross-stitch designs, and wool, felt, and leather can be striking and distinctive as well (as in the Into the Woods Fascinator on p. 127).

Lace, ribbons, and trims

Like a beautiful fabric, these pretty embellishments from the sewing world draw the eye within a design. Add richness, softness, or vividness with the right addition of trim, whether it's an estate sale treasure or a crisp new favorite from the fabric store. I loved using two scraps of vintage hem lace to make a fabric flower (see p. 122), but it would be just

Bead sizes in millimeters

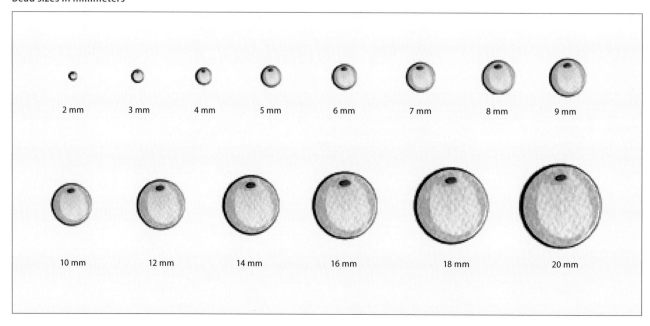

| 2 mm | 3 mm | 4 mm | 5 mm | 6 mm | 7 mm | 8 mm | 9 mm |

| 10 mm | 12 mm | 14 mm | 16 mm | 18 mm | 20 mm |

as gorgeous in new lace, ribbon, or anything else that catches your eye.

Paper

Using paper or similar ephemera is a lighthearted and fun way to add interest to your jewelry or craft projects. Acid-free cardstock, paint chips, and kraft-paper labels are all workhorses throughout the book, while special materials like washi tape or vintage stamps are a joy to work with in the right project.

Other media

Some specific pieces I really enjoyed working with for special projects are tiny Christmas trees, predrilled wooden blanks for cross-stitching or needlepoint, suede fringe for tassels, and perfect little glass jars with corks for making jewelry or decorations. Just keep your eyes open in your day-to-day life, and you'll stumble upon your own favorite components that can be worked into your designs!

VINTAGE TREASURES

I love using vintage pieces from the past in new ways, and I hope they inspire you to come up with your own favorites. I love taking inexpensive old or broken pieces apart to reuse the beads or focal points, but finding deadstock (never-used vintage materials) is wonderful, too. Here are a few tips on finding special vintage pieces.

Family pieces

If you inherit vintage costume jewelry or more valuable pieces that are broken, damaged, or unwearable, working them into your new designs can be both meaningful and joyful. My Wedding Ring Pendant (see p. 95) is a nice example of

a treasured piece that brought me a lot of happiness during the months I had to reluctantly take my wedding ring off my ring finger due to water retention during pregnancy.

Flea markets, thrift stores, or yard sales

Look for jars of buttons, bags of beads or jewelry, or individual pieces in good shape. The treasure hunt factor is a lot of fun!

Vintage and consignment shops

The jewelry cases at good vintage and secondhand shops are ever-changing, and whether it's an elegant midcentury brooch or over-the-top Dynasty-era rhinestone earrings (I personally have a special fondness for clip earrings) that could sing as a necklace, picturing these bygone pieces in a new setting can be very inspiring.

Etsy and eBay

Use careful search terms, the more specific the better, to sift through the hundreds or thousands of listings (like "vintage Lucite faceted round" rather than "vintage beads"). Most important, once you do find special pieces, bookmark or mark good shops as favorites so you can come back to them. You can also message sellers to ask if they have more or would combine beads or materials into lots rather than buying smaller quantities over and over.

Design Principles: Vintage Meets Modern

You'll see this principle, one of my favorites, illustrated throughout every project chapter in this book. One example of how you can apply this concept in your projects is to reinterpret a forlorn clip earring from a fancier era into your modern jewelry. The three pendants on pp. 116–118 are all made with one, or a pair, of clip earrings that would otherwise gather dust in an old jewelry box. Find your own ways to celebrate the best of vintage components with new and interesting framing.

STRINGING

■ **Flexible beading wire** (like Soft Flex®) is a coated wire that comes in many thicknesses, from super-thin to heavy, depending on what you're stringing. It's durable, supple, and great for heavier beads or pendants—and the bonus is that you don't need to use a needle to make your designs.

■ **Crimp beads** can be used to finish the ends of your flexible wire pieces. Smooth sterling silver or gold-filled crimp beads are much higher quality than base metal, which has rough edges that can damage your cord over time.

■ **Silk beading cord** in various thicknesses is perfect for knotting between beads. Good-quality silk cord comes prethreaded on a flexible needle, so you can get started right away. And **pearl cotton** is wonderful for cross-stitch or other decorative stitching.

■ **Beading boards and trays** make creating your own pieces so much easier—you can look at beads, charms, and materials in different combinations before making your final choices.

NEEDLES

Use a twisted wire or beading needle with most thin cord or thread. Remember, you'll need to use a needle with an eye that can accommodate your cord but can also pass through the smallest beads you're using. Twisted wire needles are handy because the eye collapses as you pass it through a bead, and they're available in thin or thicker weights depending on your other materials. Silk and nylon beading thread often comes prethreaded on a needle.

CORDS, THREADS, AND RIBBON

Here are some stringing materials that you can use on various projects throughout the book (shown on p. 9).

■ **Silk cord** is wonderful to knot on, especially for softer or smoother beads, like pearls, glass, or less brittle semiprecious stones. It has a lovely drape in a finished piece. Always stretch the cord before using, since it will give later if you don't. If you choose the kind that comes on a card and there are noticeable kinks and folds, dampen it, then hang the cord over a hook or door overnight so it will dry straight. Silk cord comes in a range of thicknesses—make sure if you're knotting that you choose one that will easily go through your bead holes but will create a stopper when knotted to keep beads in place.

■ **Nylon and other artificial threads** are strong and resilient and will not stretch. However, they are slipperier and harder to knot. Nylon is great for hard gemstones, which can damage softer materials like silk over time.

■ **Leather or suede cording** is great to string on and has a smooth, natural drape. If the leather has a harder, smoother, more compact finish, it will likely be colorfast and largely waterproof. Leather and suede generally work well with crimp clasps.

■ **Polyester sewing thread** is what I suggest for stitching beads onto fabric or another form for embellishment. It is much more durable over time than cotton.

■ **Invisible beading thread** is clear and delicate and works wonderfully when embellishing fabric, too. It does tend to curl up and tangle a bit, so try using a little Thread Heaven Thread Conditioner and Protectant® or other conditioner on it to smooth it out nicely.

■ **Narrow ribbon** can be lovely to use—it can be easier to slip a charm or bead on if you cut the ribbon at a diagonal so it has a point much like a needle. If it frays after you've beaded with it, just trim the ribbon to a point again. I use extra-large crimp beads to finish narrow ribbon pendants.

Combining Colors

Use bold colors with delicate designs for an unexpected twist, or try sophisticated paler shades to flatter your coloring. Some fun combinations include these:

- Light blue and brown
- Pink and brown
- Pink and lime green
- Pink and olive green
- Turquoise and lime green
- Turquoise and yellow
- Turquoise and olive green

- Orange and olive green
- Orange and blue
- Dark red and pink
- Dark red and light blue
- Plum and lavender
- Plum and turquoise
- Dark blue and turquoise

- Black and anything (especially pinks, reds, and light blues)
- Clear and anything
- White and anything

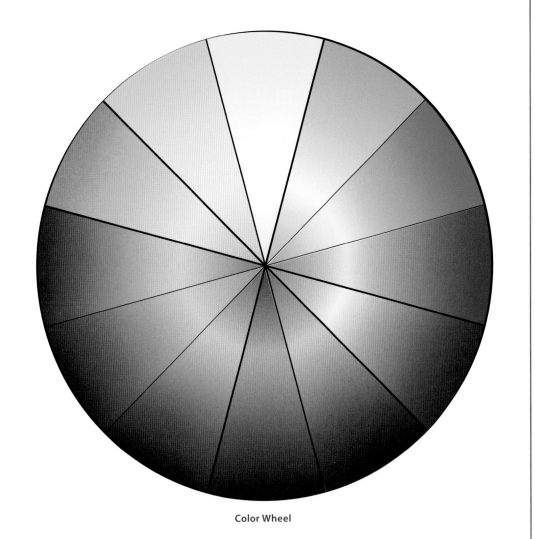

Color Wheel

DESIGN

The 120 projects in this book range from beginner-friendly to involved and elaborate, and they employ quite a few techniques. Try using different sizes and colors of beads or different materials than the ones pictured for distinctive effects. Here are a few ideas to get you started creating your own unique variations and designs.

Leaving spaces within your jewelry designs can give a modern look, which is easy to wear with anything from a cocktail dress to a T-shirt and jeans. Space also gives you room to appreciate each component, since they're not jumbled together. Busier, more crowded pieces can be striking, too, but they tend to dominate what you're wearing.

Mixing different-size beads within a design can make it really pop, while using the same size throughout lends more of a classic feel—think of your grandmother's pearls.

A simple but effective rule is to design in threes (or ones, or fives)—odd numbers of beads make a gorgeous, symmetrical design. Think of one large bead in the middle of a necklace between two smaller ones, or five identical beads spaced along a choker.

If you do use two beads, it can be eye-catching to vary the size or spacing so the beads are offset instead of symmetrical.

Each project has at least two variations shown to give you ideas for personalizing your own pieces.

COLOR

You can create striking color combinations by choosing a color from the color wheel and pairing it with a variation of its opposite (see p. 15). Try using orange with blue or a deep red with an olive green—making the green more neutral will make sure it doesn't look like Christmas!

Colors that are closely related can work well together, too. Create a monochromatic design in different hues, like hot pink next to a lighter pink, or a range of bright and dark blues in a single piece.

Try mixing less-expected pairings or combining two brighter colors with neutrals or metallics for a gorgeous effect. Black or clear beads go with anything, of course. Go a little easier on neons and difficult pairings like bright yellow and purple—those could look stunning with a very similar color mix, or with metals and neutrals.

These barrettes allow plenty of options for personality. For instructions, see p. 139.

Design Principles

Throughout this book, you'll find little sidebars that I've called "Design Principles." These are little themes that I often keep in mind when I am designing my jewelry projects, and I hope they will be helpful to you. Here are the design principles that I've explained, and exactly where you'll find more about each of them. What other design ideas do you keep in mind when you're creating your own jewelry and accessories?

Vintage Meets Modern (p. 13)

Botanicals (p. 66)

Somewhere for the Eye to Land (p. 97)

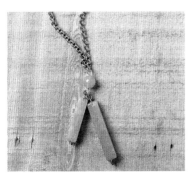
Elongated vs. Compact (p. 103)

Mixing High and Low Materials (p. 132)

Mixing Metals (p. 142)

Color, Color, Color! (p. 150)

Negative Space (p. 154)

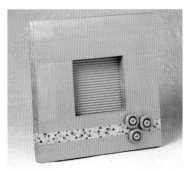
Graphic and Linear (p. 174)

Stringing, Wirework, Stitching, and Repair

Here are the techniques you'll use to create every design in this book. You may need to practice some of them a few times before trying them out on a project, but they get much easier with a little trial and error.

BEAD STRINGING

Bead stringing is the most basic way to construct a piece of jewelry like a necklace or bracelet—just thread a needle or pick up a piece of flexible wire, secure the end, and add beads one after another. Depending on what you're using for materials and your own taste, there are several ways to construct your piece of jewelry.

NEEDLE BEADING

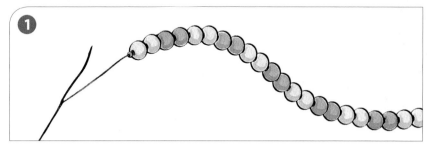

Needle beading

1. Before you begin, you may want to add a bead tip (see p. 20) to add a clasp or end component.

2. Thread a needle with thin material (like elastic, silk cord, or nylon thread), and tie a knot or cover the end with a doubled piece of tape.

3. Add beads one (or more) at a time, and continue beading until you reach the desired length.

4. Finish with a bead tip or durable knotting (if no clasp is required).

Finishing with bead tips

Bead tips cover a knot at each end of the cord securely, and the curved hook attaches to a finding. See complete instructions for knotting on p. 30.

1. Tie a knot near the beginning of the cord and slip one bead tip onto it, with the two cupping halves facing and enveloping the knot (as shown). Knot again directly above the bead tip to keep it in place.

2. String or knot the beads as you go until you're finished with the piece. Tie a knot at the end.

3. Add a bead tip with the halves facing outward, away from the beads and toward the needle. Using tweezers to pinpoint the spot, tie a knot inside the tip and pull it taut.

4. Add a drop of glue or Fray Check™ (I often use Fray Check, then glue), and snip the cord ends away just above each knot.

5. Using flat-nose pliers, press the tips closed around the knots.

6. Using round-nose pliers, curve the hook around a jump ring or clasp loop.

FINISHING WITH BEAD TIPS

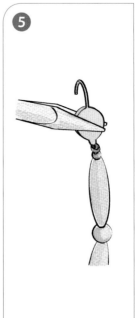

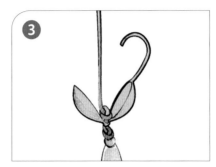

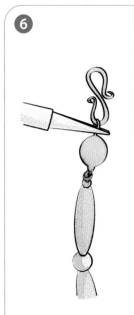

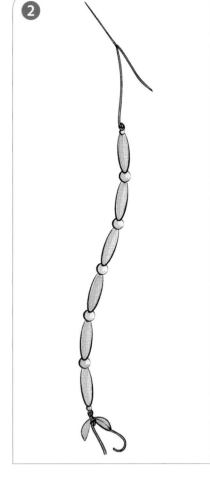

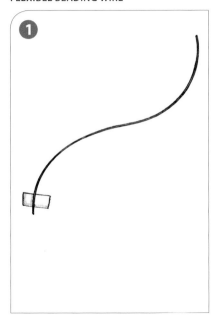

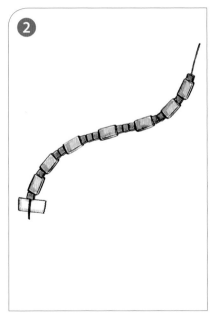

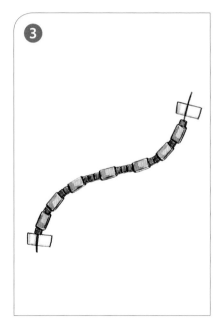

Flexible beading wire

This thin, durable wire is easy to bead with. Use good-quality materials—it's so worth it! I highly recommend Soft Flex wire, since inexpensive tiger tail wire kinks and ages poorly.

1. Cut a piece of wire at least 4 in. to 6 in. longer than the finished length of the piece you're making. Add a doubled piece of clear tape near the end of the wire to hold your design as you string the pieces—it's easy to take off when you're ready to finish the ends but won't kink or untie itself as a knot often does.

2. Begin creating your design from one end, or construct the middle section and move outward—it's up to you. Beads will slip right onto the wire, so you don't need a needle. Just add them in the desired pattern, and remember, you can always tape the working end and switch back to the other side if you want to change your design—it's very flexible.

3. If you need to take a break or don't finish the project right away, just tape both ends of the wire to hold the pattern.

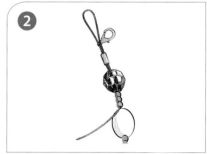

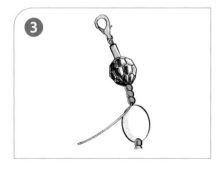

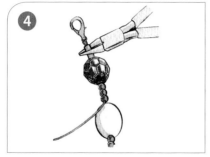

Crimp beads

Finish a Soft Flex wire or ribbon piece with crimp beads—small metal cylinders that hold a doubled cord securely when you flatten or crimp them with pliers. They can also be used to hold a bead or piece in place on a single wire or cord or as a design element. I recommend sterling or gold-filled cylinder-shaped crimp beads, which are easy to work with and finish smoothly. Base metal crimps can be rough at the edge, scratching your skin or cutting through the wire itself.

1. Finish stringing your piece. Place a single crimp bead on the end of the strand and add a clasp.

2. Slip the wire tail back through the crimp bead, then through the next several beads.

3. Tug the wire so it's taut, with no gaps between beads or at the end.

4. Firmly crimp the bead closed with flat-nose pliers.

5. Clip off the end of the wire close to the beads so the end tucks back in and won't scratch your skin.

Crimp clasps

You'll attach all-in-one crimp/clasp pieces similarly. Just use flat-nose pliers to securely flatten the metal crimp around the cord or ribbon. Crimp one side at a time if it's a flap style or the entire thing if it's a cylinder style. You may want to add a drop of glue to the cord before slipping it into the crimp clasp for extra hold. Your local bead store can help you choose the perfect crimp end for the cord.

WIREWORK

These basic techniques—forming plain loops and wrapped loops with pliers—are easy steps that transform a simple piece of wire into a custom eyepin, earring wire, chain link, or pendant. Plain and wrapped loops are the knit and purl stitches of jewelry making—they're invaluable for making just about anything, from simple drop earrings to elaborate wire masterpieces. Once you learn these basics, you'll be able to repair or alter jewelry and create and embellish new pieces.

In these diagrams, the flat-nose pliers are shown with blue handles, the round-nose pliers have red handles, and the wire cutters have black handles.

Tip: If you're new to wirework, you can practice these techniques on a bigger scale using pipe cleaners. The forgiving, flexible pipe cleaners are an easy way to learn the precise shaping and coiling that make a successful loop or connector.

Variation: Flat-Front Plain Loop

For this variation, the plain loop looks like a "P"—the curve of the loop is to the back of, say, a drop pendant. To do this, skip step 1 and grasp the end of the wire. Simply curve it into a loop. The wire will still look straight and smooth in front instead of obviously curved.

PLAIN LOOPS

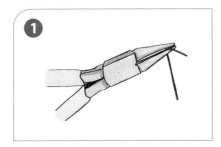

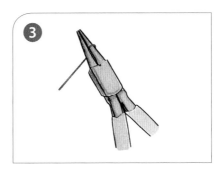

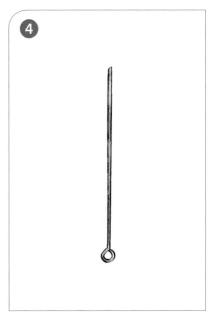

Plain loops

1. Cut a 4-in. piece of craft wire, then use flat-nose pliers to bend it at a neat 90-degree angle about ¼ in. to ½ in. from the end. The longer the wire bend, the larger the loop.

2. Holding the longer part of the wire with the flat-nose pliers, grasp the end of the shorter wire bend with the tip of the round-nose pliers.

3. Twist your wrist so you begin to bring the very end of the wire around to meet the bend, forming a neat circle. You'll essentially be rolling the pliers toward you. It can be easier to do this in two steps, letting go of the wire about

halfway through and then grasping it again with the pliers to finish bringing it around. You can adjust or finish the loop after you curve the wire so it's perfectly round.

4. The finished loop should look like a lollipop. If there is any excess wire extending beyond the circle, trim it with wire cutters and gently tweak it back into shape. If the loops are misshapen or crooked, just clip them off and start again.

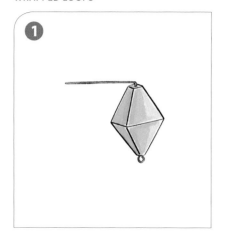

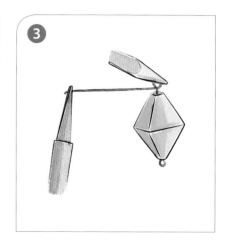

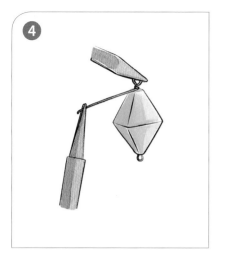

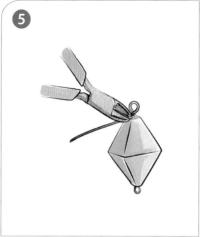

Tip: Practice with inexpensive craft wire until your loops are nice and even.

Plain loops work best with thick wire (such as 20 gauge), while the more secure wrapped loops are good for thinner wire (24 gauge) but can also work well with thicker gauges, too.

Wrapped loops

1. Place a bead on the eyepin you've just created. Grasp the wire just above the bead with round-nose pliers, and make another neat 90-degree angle bend above and over the tips, holding the wire tail with flat-nose pliers.

2. Next, adjust the round-nose pliers so they are gripping on either side of the wire bend, above and below it. Use the flat-nose pliers to pull the wire tail over the end of the round-nose pliers and all the way around, creating a circle with an extra tail of wire still extending beyond it.

3. Use the flat-nose pliers to hold the circle while you grip the end of the wire tail with the round-nose pliers.

4. Wrap the wire tail around the space above the bead, working from top to bottom to create a neat coil, and stop when you reach the top of the bead. If the wire coils on top of itself or starts to get messy, stop coiling and unwind it, then start again, going more slowly this time. If it's really tangled or kinked, you can always start over with a new piece.

5. Clip the end of the wire flush with the coil. Make sure the sharp edge isn't sticking out—if it is, use flat-nose pliers to flatten and smooth it into the coil.

Basic dangle

Creating a plain loop below a bead and a wrapped loop above it transforms the bead into a dangling charm, as illustrated above.

Alternatively, use a headpin or eyepin for the base instead of forming the plain loop.

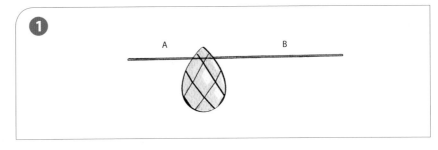

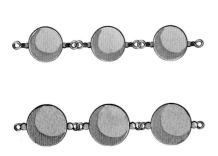

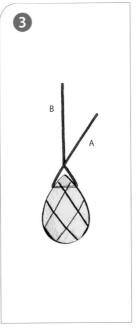

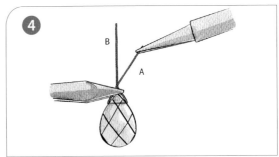

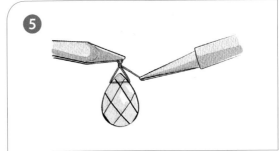

Double-looped bead connector

Use this process to link a bead into a longer chain or design. Just cut a piece of wire and make a wrapped loop or a plain loop on each side, being sure to join the loops to the chain or design before you close them completely. As always, you'll use a wrapped loop with a thinner-gauge wire (24 and up) and have the option of doing a plain loop with a heavier-gauge wire (20 and below). See the illustrations above.

Briolette wrapping

This technique is great for creating a handmade "hanger" for both horizontally drilled briolettes and pieces with a space in the middle. It's essentially a variation on the double-wrapped loop on p. 26.

1. Cut a 4-in. piece of wire and run it through a briolette, side to side, so one-third of the wire is on one side (A) and two-thirds on the other (B).

2. Fold one wire, then the other, up into a triangle, following the lines of the bead. The wires will look like an X.

3. Form a sharp angle in wire B so it extends straight above the bead.

4. Grip the wires below the X with flat-nose pliers, and wrap wire A in a coil around wire B. Stop after three coils and clip the wire.

5. Form a loop above the coil. Grip it with flat-nose pliers, using round-nose pliers to make a new coil starting at the top and moving downward.

6. Bring the wire tail around to the side of the coil where the tail from step 4 is and clip it closely. Use the flat-nose pliers to make sure the wire clipping is flush with the coil. This side will be the back of the finished piece, so the neat coiling shows continuously and the raw edges are hidden behind it.

Variation: Side-to-Side Briolette

Use this version to connect a single briolette to a chain or cord on both sides, instead of making a drop to suspend from one strand. Cut a piece of wire and make a wrapped loop on one side, slipping it through the last link of a piece of chain before completing the wrap. Slip the briolette onto the wire and form a second wrapped loop on its other side, again adding it to a last link of chain before completing the wrap (see the drawing below). You may want to curve the loops upward or leave them perfectly straight.

Double-wrapped loop

This dual loop wraps around (or through) a charm or piece and the chain or cord to form a double connector or hanger. It's made the same way as a double-looped bead connector without the bead in the middle of the coils.

1. Cut a piece of wire and form a briolette-style hanger around or through the piece, front to back, leaving the top loop open after forming the first half. You'll wrap the coil using the back wire tail, going around the front piece.

2. Slip the open loop onto a chain or cord and complete the wrap, making sure the wire ends are tucked to the back of the coil so they don't show. As you wind the top wrap, the coil will stay neater if you bring the wire around on the opposite side from the first wrap.

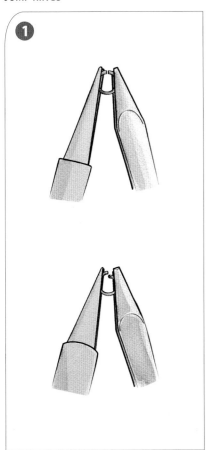

Jump rings

Use jump rings—small circles of wire with an opening—to attach clasps, suspend charms, or form a simple chain.

1. Open a jump ring by gripping the ring on each side with a pair of pliers. Separate the ring by tilting the right side toward you and the left side away from you—don't pull the ring open into a U-shape.

2. Close the ring by reversing step 1. The ring should close neatly with no gap where the ends meet. If it doesn't meet neatly on the first try, gently tilt the two sides back and forth past the closed position a few times until the ring "clicks" shut.

You can also make sure it's secure by squeezing it shut with the flat-nose pliers.

To attach a clasp to a chain, simply slip both the last link in the chain and the clasp (or its ring) onto the open jump ring in step 1. Close it to connect the two, as in step 2.

To attach a charm to a chain, choose the link you want to use and open a jump ring. Slip the charm or dangle onto the ring, then slip one end of the open ring through the link you've chosen. Close it securely.

To create a simple chain, just join a series of jump rings into a long row. Start with two: Open one, join it to the other, and close it. Add a third the same way, and so on until the chain is the desired length.

Tip: If your jump ring becomes misshapen or dented from plier marks, just throw it away and start over with a new one.

Eyepins

These are ultra-simple—just take a 1-in. to 4-in. piece of straight wire and form a plain loop at one end. That's it!

Clasps

Use round-nose pliers to bend wire into clasp shapes, much like heavier-gauge versions of earring wires (see below). Pair these handmade clasps with soldered rings.

Make different sizes of clasps by changing the length of the wire piece you work with. A 1½-in. wire will make an approximately ⅝-in. hook clasp, for example, and a 2-in. wire will make a ¾-in. S-clasp.

Hooks

1. Cut a 1½-in. to 2-in. piece of 16-gauge or 18-gauge wire. Following the natural curve of the wire, bend a curve into it just before the halfway point.

2. Form a small or medium-size plain loop at the shorter end, curving the wire out into a circle. This will be the hook end.

3. Now form a larger plain loop at the longer end. This loop will connect to the cord, chain, or jump ring.

4. Open the larger plain loop just as you would open a jump ring to attach it to the finding or chain.

HOOKS

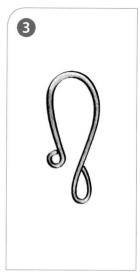

BASIC EARRING WIRES

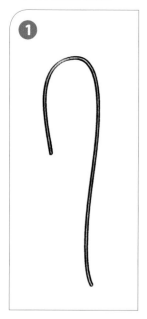
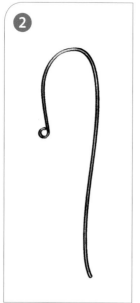

Basic earring wires

1. Cut a 2½-in. piece of 22-gauge or 24-gauge wire, and form a large, round curve starting about ¾ in. from the end. If the wire has a natural curve, follow it.

2. Next, create a small flat-front plain loop at the short end. This will be the loop of the earring wire.

3. Use pliers to make a neat bend on the long end of the wire.

S-clasp

1. Cut a 2-in. piece of 16-gauge or 18-gauge half-hard wire. Hold the wire about one-third of the way in on one side and make a curve in it, following the natural curve of the wire.

2. Make a second curve about one-third of the way in from the other side. Now you have a basic S-shape (as shown at right).

3. Form a small plain loop first at one end of the S (the flat-front variation is fine, since the thicker wire will be harder to bend) and then the other.

4. Use pliers to adjust the wire so one side is closed and the other is slightly open—this side will be the hook, and the closed side will be the connector.

S-CLASP

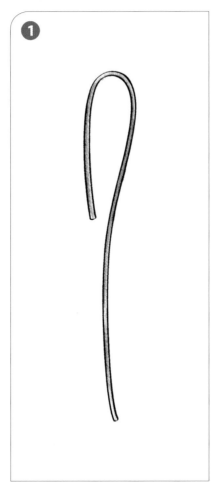

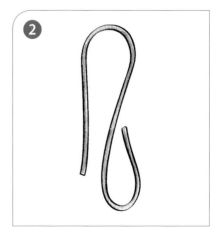

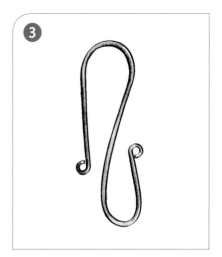

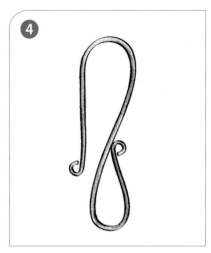

KNOTTING

Knotting between beads is easy—especially when you use narrow tweezers to pinpoint exactly where you want your knot to go. Use knotting to separate beads or to create spaces on a cord.

1. Choose where you want the knot to be, and grip that spot firmly with tweezers.

2. Bring the working cord around and over to tie a simple square knot over the tip of the tweezers.

3. Move the tweezers away just as you tighten the knot closed. You can also use a row of knots to hold a larger piece.

KNOTTING

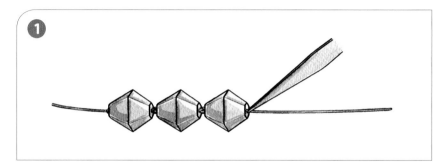

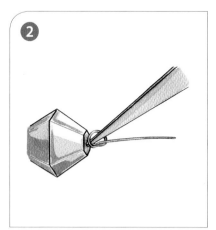

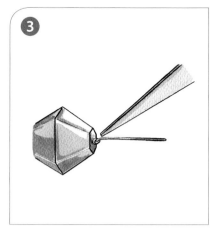

STITCHING

You can stitch beads, buttons, and charms onto fabric and ribbons as easily as threading a needle.

Running stitch

This simple forward stitch is the easiest way to join two pieces of fabric or make a broken-line design for decoration.

1. Thread a needle and bring it up from the back (wrong side) of the fabric through to the front so the knot is on the underside.

2. Next, just stitch ahead, moving the needle forward as shown in the drawing at right, following the pattern

RUNNING STITCH

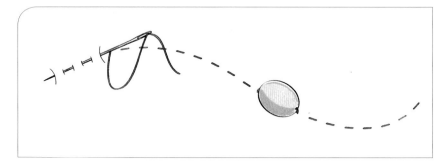

of your choice—straight, curved, or angled. You can easily vary the length or distance between your stitches to change their look.

Bead stitching

1. Thread a needle with thread or cord and double the thread tail. Tie a knot at the end.

2. Choose where you want to place the first bead, then bring the needle up from the wrong side of the fabric there to hide the knot. Slip the bead onto the needle and all the way down the thread. Let the bead lie flat on the fabric, and bring the needle back through the fabric to hold it in place.

3. Bring the thread through the bead twice more for security, always pulling the thread taut as you sew. If you are using a charm or other decoration on your project (like the Three Rings Handbag on p. 180), stitch it on using openings in the overall layout—invisible thread is great for these pieces. Stitch sequins on through their center holes or as their design dictates; layering beads over sequins is also a lovely approach (as shown in the Sequin Flowers Handbag on p. 181).

4. Place the second bead in your design, and repeat steps 2 and 3 to stitch it down. Continue until all the beads are in place, then knot securely on the back of your work.

For projects like Briolette Flower Clips (p.123) that use a flat piece rather than a round bead, you'll use a variation of this technique—simply repeat 2–3 stitches in the same spot through the hole in your piece to secure it to fabric.

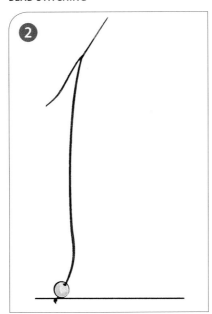

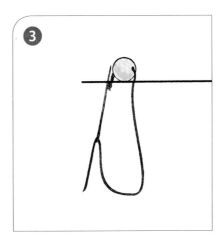

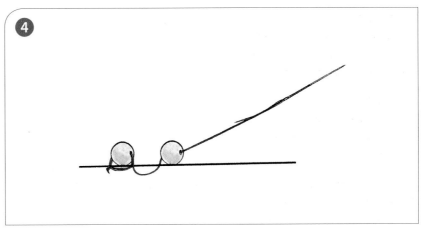

Tip: *If you are stitching the beads on with sewing thread (especially nice when you want to match your garment or ribbon's unusual color exactly), be sure to use 100 percent polyester thread instead of cotton, which is much less durable. For added resilience, cut your thread, run it through beeswax twice, and give it a quick iron (on the synthetic setting) to seal it. This process will strengthen your thread considerably. Match your bead weight to the fabric or object you're embellishing—a thin material will sag with heavy beads attached, so use lighter-weight or smaller beads instead.*

Cross-Stitching

This simple decorative stitch pattern looks wonderful as a geometric or graphic design on gridded fabric or, in our projects, wooden blanks. The front will show your clean, repetitive rows of Xs, while the back with its stitching and thread tail will be hidden behind a neat layer of felt in the two cross-stitched projects in this book (p. 114 and p. 130). In both projects, I recommend starting at the outer edge of your wooden blank, as shown in the diagrams. You can also make individual Xs one by one, but it's faster to make half-stitches across a row, then double back to finish them with the second half-stitch.

1. Thread a needle (I like to use one strand of pearl cotton, but you can use two strands of embroidery floss) and bring it up from the back (wrong side) of the wooden blank, into the hole at the left upper corner of the piece (A). Leave a tail of a couple of inches at the back and do not knot it.

2. Bring the needle diagonally across to the hole one to the right and one down from the start (B) and pass it through to the back again. This is your first half-stitch.

3. Bring the needle back through the hole just above B, catching the thread tail at the back, and repeat step 2 to form another half-stitch next to the first one. Continue until you reach the other end of the top row and have filled it with diagonal half-stitches, securing the thread tail securely.

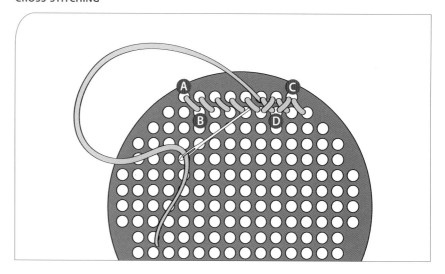

4. Now bring the needle up and through to hole (C). Pull the thread through so it's taut.

5. Bring the needle diagonally across to the lower corner to form an ✕ (D).

6. Continue to complete the first row of cross-stitches across the top of the wooden blank. Continue around the perimeter of the blank the same way, filling the rows in neatly and bringing your needle through several stitches on the back to "knot" it. Change colors to create a pattern inside the outer rim.

JEWELRY REPAIR

Let's face it—jewelry can be fragile. Whether it's a new or vintage piece, you can often repair or rework a break or damaged section. Another option is to rework the best of the existing piece into a whole new design—be creative in recycling a single earring or broken brooch into the centerpiece or highlight of an updated piece.

JEWELRY REPAIR

Mending a chain

To mend a broken chain, you'll first need to cut away the damaged links. Sometimes it's easiest to just start over with a new length of chain and add the clasp and other components to it to rebuild your piece.

You can often match a jump ring to your chain links for a subtle fix, as shown in the top right drawing. Another option is to connect your chain using a linked coordinating bead, shown in the bottom right drawing. You can add them symmetrically so the join isn't as obvious once you've added to the design in more than one place.

Replacing a jump ring

This is an easy repair. When a jump ring has deteriorated, simply cut it loose and replace it with a similar new one. If your piece has many jump rings (a link bracelet or necklace, for example), carefully examine the others to make sure that they're still in good shape. It's easy to replace one before it gets worn out instead of doing a fix on the fly while you're out and about wearing your jewelry.

Converting a piece into a pendant

You can glue a bail onto the back of a flat-backed button, bead, or pin and wear it as a pendant. Be sure that you attach the bail to a clean, dry surface and that your hardware is heavy enough to support the weight of the pendant.

Reknotting

Unfortunately, this is a complete do-over; you'll have to cut the beads free and reknot them on a new cord from scratch. If you lost any beads in the shuffle and they're hard to match, try adding extras on both sides of the piece so they're less obvious.

Gluing

See the glue descriptions on pp. 5–6 for advice on which glue to use for your project. Remember, always let the glue dry completely and make sure the two surfaces you're joining are clean and dry. Use very good ventilation when working with any toxic or strong glues.

Painting

Follow any directions given for your brand of paint, and be sure to work on a protected surface (like newspaper or wax paper). I always use at least two coats—sometimes more—letting one dry completely before adding the next. The project descriptions offer more specific advice.

The Projects

Pop of Color Earrings

▶ **TECHNIQUES:**

Wrapped Loops Orange Crush Earrings / **Plain Loops** Orange Crush Earrings, Earth Tone Tassel Earrings / **Gluing** Earth Tone Tassel Earrings / **Painting** Sunset Earrings

This monochromatic style delivers a pop of beautiful color in a simple little package. Mix beads and elements of different shapes and sizes into a striking arrangement that you'll love wearing. Since the colors are so similar, I like to mix faceted and smooth pieces together in the same design to add visual contrast and texture. Use any color you're most drawn to for these earrings!

Orange Crush Earrings

● ○ ○ **EASY**

I love the simplicity of pairing a small bead with a larger one so they complement each other. Using a mix of opaque and translucent or faceted and smooth beads gives beautiful contrast, too.

▼ **YOU'LL NEED**

Pliers

24-gauge wire or four headpins

Two small beads (I used faceted Lucite rounds)

Two large beads (I used smooth opaque flat circles)

Pair of earring wires

FINISHED SIZE

2 in.

1. Cut two 3-in. pieces and two 2-in. pieces of wire and form a plain loop at the end of each one (or use headpins).

2. Slip one small bead onto each of the shorter wires and form a wrapped loop above each, creating two small bead dangles.

3. Repeat with the larger beads and the longer wires, creating two large bead dangles.

4. Open the earring wires' loops. Place a large bead dangle on the first wire, followed by a small bead dangle. Close the earring wire. Repeat to make the second earring.

Earth Tone Tassel Earrings

● ○ ○ **EASY**

This simple design mixes texture and color in a beautiful palette of earth tones, suspending handmade suede fringe tassels below a pair of smooth beads. The tassels are remarkably easy to make! Vary the lengths or colors for a totally different look (see the Tassels on Chain botanical décor project on p. 163 for another way to embellish a project with tassels).

▼ **YOU'LL NEED**

Pliers

Two eyepins

20-gauge wire

Four beads (two for each earring)

7-in. by 2-in. piece of suede fringe

Pair of earring wires

Glue

FINISHED SIZE

4½ in.

1. Create tassels by cutting the suede fringe into two 3½-in.-wide pieces. Set them flat on your worksurface.

2. Place an eyepin at one end of the first fringe piece, with the round "eye" surfacing just above the top edge, and add glue. Begin rolling the fringe into a spiral so that the eyepin is tucked neatly inside the center, adding dabs of glue as you roll the fringe. Finish the first tassel by carefully gluing the far end of the fringe down, so the tassel is symmetrical, neat, and smooth. The loop of the eyepin should be centered above the tassel for hanging.

3. Repeat step 2 to make the other tassel with the second piece of fringe and eyepin. Allow both tassels to dry completely.

4. Cut four pieces of wire, each about 1 in. longer than the beads, and form each bead into a connector with plain loops on either side of it.

5. Arrange two beads above the tassel to help decide on your design. Once you're happy with it, begin joining the bead connectors by carefully opening a plain loop, slipping another connector's loop into it and then closing it securely. Join the tassel below the lower bead the same way.

6. Add earring wires above the upper bead and close them securely.

Sunset Earrings
by Torie Nguyen

● ● ○ **INTERMEDIATE**

These sunset-inspired earrings pair a beautiful base color with smooth metallic paint for an impactful circle design. You can easily make them with the same supplies as the Sunset Chandelier Necklace (see p. 75) and have endless possibilities for customizing them!

▼ YOU'LL NEED

Pliers

One paint chip from the hardware store

1¼-in. circle paper punch

¹⁄₁₆-in. tiny hole punch

Washi tape or paper tape

Gold spray paint

Acrylic paint for accents

Paintbrush

Pair of earring wires

Dropcloth

FINISHED SIZE

1½ in.

1. Using the circle paper punch, punch out two 1¼-in. circles from the paint chip.

2. With the washi tape or paper tape, cover the area on the circles that you do not want spray-painted.

3. Lay out a dropcloth in a well-ventilated area.

4. Optional step: Place the circles right side down and spray one light coat of paint on the backs. Allow to dry. (If you want to leave the backs the way they are, skip this step.)

5. Lay the circles right side up on the dropcloth. Spray them evenly with one coat of spray paint and allow to dry. If desired, paint a second coat and allow to dry.

Carefully remove the tape from the circles.

6. Dip the top end (not the brush end) of the paintbrush into the acrylic paint and make dots or other patterns on the circles. Allow to dry.

7. Decide which part is the top of the circles and punch a ¹⁄₁₆-in. hole near the top edge.

8. With pliers, open the loop on the earring wires by gently twisting the loop away from you. Place one circle on each earring wire and close the loops with the opposite motion that you used to open them.

Tip: For a variation, cut the washi tape into different shapes to mask off fun patterns. Create longer dangles by hanging the circles from some chain or linking multiple circles together with jump rings.

Just a Little Sparkle Earrings

▶ **TECHNIQUES:**

Plain Loops Loop-d-Loop Earrings / **Wrapped Loops** Vintage Tinsel Earrings, Sparkle Tassel Earrings / **Bead Stringing** Loop-d-Loop Earrings, Sparkle Tassel Earrings / **Crimp Beads** Loop-d-Loop Earrings

All three of these earrings include lovely sparkly elements within an overall design, so your eye follows the sparkle and shine.

Each project also uses an elongated arrangement, so the light and colors sweep up and down for an elegant and eye-catching—but very wearable—finished design.

Loop-d-Loop Earrings

● ● ○ **INTERMEDIATE**

The teardrop loops in this design echo one another, spotlighting a set of pretty vintage faceted beads. I combined a single vintage bead on the smaller curve with the three just below it and radiated complementary smaller beads outward from each center, but any repeating pattern you prefer will work nicely.

▼ **YOU'LL NEED**

Pliers

Soft Flex wire

Two crimp beads

Eight vintage beads of your choice

28 complementary beads of your choice (I used small oval beads)

Seed beads

Pair of earring wires

Tape

FINISHED SIZE

3 in.

1. Cut two 5-in. and two 7-in. pieces of Soft Flex wire. Starting with a 5-in. piece, create a repeating 2½-in.-long pattern of beads with a vintage bead in the center. I alternated between seed beads and smaller oval beads radiating out from my center vintage bead. When you like your design, add tape to both ends of the Soft Flex wire to hold the beads in place. Make an identical loop with the second 5-in. piece of wire. This will be the smaller inner loop.

2. Create a 4-in.-long repeating bead pattern on the 7-in. piece of wire that also radiates out from the center. This will be the longer outer loop. I placed three of my vintage beads in the center (separated by one seed bead between each), then radiated outward with the same repeating pattern from my first loop. When you're happy with the design, add tape to the edges, then create an identical loop with the second 7-in. piece of wire.

3. Holding one shorter loop and one longer loop together by the ends, remove the tape and pass all four wire ends through a crimp bead, gently pulling tightly so the beads hang smoothly with no loose areas.

4. Carefully pass the two wires on the right back down through the crimp bead to form a small upper loop. Thread those wire ends into the first couple of beads on the left side.

5. Place one tip of a round-nose pliers through that small upper loop to hold it in place, and use your fingers to gently tug the two wire ends you just threaded to make sure the upper loop is neat and the two teardrop loops of the design nestle neatly together. (The other two wire ends should still extend upward.) Then use flat-nose pliers to flatten the crimp bead, making sure the flat section faces forward.

6. Repeat steps 3, 4, and 5 to make the second earring. Trim the excess Soft Flex wire tails with the cutter. Open the earring wires, place the earrings on, and close them securely.

Vintage Tinsel Earrings

 EASY

I found these beautiful round vintage Lucite beads with strands of real gold tinsel embedded inside and knew they would be gorgeous earrings. I love how they sparkle when they catch the light, paired with small pearl and filigree circle drops for movement and contrast.

▼ YOU'LL NEED

Pliers

24-gauge wire

Two headpins

Two focal beads (I used 18-mm round Lucite beads with tinsel inside)

Four seed beads

Two 5-mm pearls

Metal filigree circles that fit nicely with the pearls

Pair of leverback earring wires

FINISHED SIZE

2¹⁄₂ in.

1. Slip each pearl onto a headpin and form a plain loop above each of them. Nestle the pearl and the filigree circle together.

2. Cut two pieces of wire, each 4 in. long, and form a wrapped loop at one end of each. Add a seed bead, a focal bead, and another seed bead to each, and then form a wrapped loop on the other side of the beads, slipping the pearl and filigree drop onto the loop before you wrap the coil.

3. Add earring wires above each earring dangle.

Sparkle Tassel Earrings
by Lynzee Malsin

● ● ●   **ADVANCED**

These tassel earrings mix sparkly bicone crystal beads at the ends of longer strands of tiny seed beads for a lovely effect. Lynzee's project is effortless to customize with the colors or sparkles you love best!

▼ **YOU'LL NEED**

Pliers

Two or more colors of size 11/0 seed beads

Two size 8/0 seed beads

Two metal cones

8 in. of 22-gauge or 24-gauge wire

Pair of earring wires

Size D Nymo® beading thread

Size 12 beading needles

Five 4-mm bicone crystals

Watch crystal cement (such as G-S Hypo Cement) or other glue

FINISHED SIZE

4½ in.

1. Cut the 24- or 22-gauge wire into two 4-in. pieces. Create a wrapped loop with one piece of wire.

2. Thread a beading needle with about 1 yd. of beading thread.

3. Knot the end of the beading thread directly to the wrapped loop.

4. String size 11/0 seed beads in colors of your choice onto the beading thread. Keep track of how many of each color you are using and write that down.

5. When you have a desired length of strung seed beads, add a size 8/0 bead, a crystal bicone, and a size 11/0 bead. String back up through the beads, skipping the bottom-most bead, which will act as an anchor for the piece of fringe you are creating. When you reach the top of the fringe piece, knot the thread once again to the top loop where you began.

6. Repeat steps 2–5 to string four more fringe pieces, varying the number of beads in each strand. Each time you complete a fringe piece, knot it the same way to the wire-wrapped loop, making it secure and durable.

7. Once you finish the five beaded fringe strands and make your final knot onto the wire-wrapped loop, place a dab of glue on the final knot. Add another dab of glue to the beginning knot as well.

8. Slip the cone onto the wire, obscuring the knots and the wire loop. Make a second wire-wrapped loop on top of the cone and attach an earring wire to that loop, as shown in the photo.

9. Repeat steps 1–8 to make a second earring the same way.

Tip: A fabulous trick for seed beading is to pass the Nymo thread through some beeswax in order to condition, soften, and protect the thread from dreadful knotting mid-project. Wax your thread before threading it onto the needle.

Nature-Inspired Earrings

▶ **TECHNIQUES:**

Bead Stringing Pearls & Petals Earrings / **Wrapped Loops** Floral Charm Drop Earrings, Filigree Leaves Earrings / **Plain Loops** Filigree Leaves Earrings

For each of these three earring designs, I was inspired by florals—pretty, feminine, and timeless. Whether you're drawn to lighthearted charms, intricate molded Lucite pieces, or filigree leaves, the beauty and simplicity of flowers and leaves translated into jewelry is always striking.

1. Open the bottom loop on each of a pair of eyepins and slip a floral charm onto each loop, closing it securely. Place a bead onto each eyepin and form a wrapped loop above it.

2. Open the earring wires and slip the top loop of the bead and charm earring onto each one. Close them securely. (Note: I used a simple hoop design here, but you can also use a more traditional earring wire.)

Pearls & Petals Earrings

● ○ ○ **EASY**

This ultra-simple design uses paddle-shaped earring wires. The wide, flat ends become a natural stopper to suspend the two elements together. Just make sure that the beads and flowers you choose can move around the curve of the earring wire.

▼ **YOU'LL NEED**

Two acrylic or Lucite flower pieces, center-drilled

Two pearls or other beads of your choice

Pair of paddle earring wires

Glue

FINISHED SIZE

2¹⁄₂ in.

Floral Charm Drop Earrings

● ○ ○ **EASY**

This simple pairing of elongated vintage glass beads and floral charms makes a pretty pair of earrings. I liked the contrast between the faceted olive green glass and the three-dimensional gold floral charm, but any flower design would be lovely.

▼ **YOU'LL NEED**

Pliers

Two floral charms with a loop at the top

Two beads that complement the charms

Two eyepins

Pair of earring wires (I used a pair of simple gold-filled round hoops)

FINISHED SIZE

3 in.

1. Slip a flower piece onto a paddle earring wire with petals facing up. Gently tug the piece downward until it sits on the paddle securely. Add a small drop of glue at the center of the piece to hold it in place.

2. Add a bead above the flower. You can add a little glue if need be or let the bead naturally sit in place. Repeat to form a second earring.

Filigree Leaves Earrings

● ○ ○ **EASY**

These filigree leaves layer together beautifully without adding much weight or bulk, since they're cut so delicately with lots of negative space. Use any beads in earth tones or other serene colors you like to connect and embellish the leaves.

▼ YOU'LL NEED

Pliers

24-gauge wire

Four leaf filigree charms (I used two that measured 2 in. long and two that measured 1¼ in., but you can use four the same size if you prefer)

Two carnelian or other focal beads

Four small beads

Pair of earring wires

FINISHED SIZE

3 in.

1. Cut six 2-in. to 3-in. pieces of wire (depending on the size of the beads) and form plain loops above and below each bead to make them into connectors.

2. Add one focal bead connector at the top of each of the larger leaves to suspend them from the earring wires.

3. Layer the two filigree leaf charms together and think about how you'd like them to connect. I chose to place my smaller leaves about ⅓ in. from the top of the bigger leaves, and to one side so they were not symmetrical. When you decide on a design, find an open area on each of the filigree designs that you can wire through for joining.

4. Join the two filigree pieces in the spot you choose using a second set of small bead connectors. Hold the earrings up and see how you like the relationship between the two leaves—you can always change the positions.

5. Finally, add the last set of small bead connectors to the bottom sections of the leaves as embellishments.

Geometric Earrings

▶ **TECHNIQUES:**

Jump Rings Hanging Triangles Earrings, Dual Circles Earrings /
Wrapped Loops Pearl Loops Earrings / **Bead Stringing** Pearl Loops Earrings

These earrings all use striking geometric shapes for a strong, interesting design that's also easy to wear. I used two different types of circles—a hammered metal set of varying sizes and a handmade circular wire loop with round pearls—while Cathy Zwicker suspended gorgeous, sleek brass triangles from a chain.

Hanging Triangles Earrings by Cathy Zwicker

● ○ ○ **EASY**

I love the look and feel of antiqued brass—it's warm with an industrial and vintage look. Combine that with geometric shapes, and it's perfection! The length of these earrings can be modified by making the pieces of chain longer or shorter.

▼ YOU'LL NEED

Wire cutters

Pliers

8 in. of chain (I used antiqued brass 2-mm rolo chain)

Two brass triangles with holes punched in two of the corners

Six jump rings

Pair of earring wires

FINISHED SIZE

3½ in.

Tip: If your triangles don't already have holes, you can add them using hole-punch pliers, as with the Northern Lights Earrings on p. 58.

1. Use wire cutters to cut the chain into four lengths that are each 2 in. long.

2. Use pliers to open one jump ring and loop it through the hole in one corner of one of the brass triangles. With the jump ring still open, loop one end of one of the 2-in. chain lengths into the jump ring. Close the jump ring securely.

3. Repeat with another jump ring and chain length on the other side of the triangle.

4. Use the pliers to open another jump ring and feed it through the ends of each of the two chain lengths hanging off the triangle to join the chains together. While the jump ring is still open, loop the earring wire on, placing it so that the earrings hang with the correct side facing out. Close the jump ring securely. You now have one complete earring!

5. Repeat steps 2–4 to complete the second earring.

Dual Circles Earrings

● ○ ○ **EASY**

This pair of earrings comes together in just a couple of minutes once you find the right set of circles to design around. I chose lightweight hammered metal pieces with an understated finish, but circles in wood, plastic, or other materials in any colors or finishes you love would be beautiful, too. Just make sure that the two sizes you're working with are harmonious when they're hanging together.

▼ **YOU'LL NEED**

Pliers

Two ¾-in. circles

Two 1¼-in. circles

Two jump rings, big enough for both circles to move freely

Pair of earring wires

FINISHED SIZE

2½ in.

1. Arrange the first small circle over the larger one and set it down on your worksurface. Open a jump ring and slip both circles into it. Close the jump ring securely.

2. Open the earring wire and add the jump ring so the circles face front and move freely. Close the earring wire securely. (Note: If the earring wire is made so that the circles face the side rather than the front, you can add another jump ring to correct the positioning, or possibly use pliers to twist the earring wire's loop 90 degrees to adjust it.)

3. Repeat steps 1 and 2 to make the second earring.

Pearl Loops Earrings

 ● ● ○ **INTERMEDIATE**

I came up with a simple way to make my own wire circles and bead right onto them for a different take on geometry. Round costume pearls and smooth white seed beads give these a calm and classic feel, but you could use bright colors, use cubes or faceted shapes, or change the scale for a more dramatic look.

▼ **YOU'LL NEED**

Pliers

24-gauge wire

Six 6-mm costume pearls

72 seed beads in a coordinating color

Pair of earring wires

Tape

FINISHED SIZE

2 in.

1. Cut two 7-in. pieces of wire and set one aside. Tape one end of the other wire and add beads in this order: 15 seed beads, 1 pearl, 3 seed beads, 1 pearl, 3 seed beads, 1 pearl, and 15 seed beads.

2. Curve this bead arrangement into a U-shape and look at the proportions. You may want to adjust the number or placement of beads—just take them off and rebead until you love the results. Add another piece of tape to the open end to seal it.

3. Curve the beads on wire into a neat circle with the wire ends crossing at the top. Create a wrapped loop there, gently tugging the wire to make sure you have a nice, even circle with the beads sitting in place. Trim the ends at the back of the coil.

4. Slip the pearl loop onto an earring wire.

5. Repeat these steps with the second piece of wire to make the second earring.

Tip: If you make a larger-scale version of these earrings, try using 20-gauge wire and beads with larger holes so the loop can support the weight of the bigger design without warping.

Semiprecious Earrings

▶ **TECHNIQUES:**

Plain Loops Little Trio Earrings, Family Birthstone Earrings / **Wrapped Loops** Little Trio Earrings, Family Birthstone Earrings / **Briolette Wrapping** Pretty Curve Earrings

I love using a mix of smaller, more delicate semiprecious beads for these designs, since larger ones can be too heavy to wear as earrings. Whether you choose exactly the same stones for your designs or mix several together, the results are sure to be gorgeous. The birthstone earrings are special favorites of mine, and I hope you love making your own version as much as I did!

Little Trio Earrings

● ○ ○ **EASY**

I chose beautiful, tiny turquoise rondelles and a delicate chain for my earrings, but you can use any semiprecious beads you're drawn to, or play with scale for a more substantial design.

▼ **YOU'LL NEED**

Pliers

Six semiprecious beads (I used turquoise rondelles)

Six headpins or 24-gauge wire

2½ in. of fine chain

Pair of earring wires

FINISHED SIZE

2 in.

1. Cut the chain into two 1¼-in. sections, one for each earring.

2. Slip a bead onto each headpin (or, if using wire, cut six 3-in. sections and form a plain loop at one end of each). Set aside four of the beads on headpins and form the first half of a wrapped loop above two of them.

3. Slip one bead dangle onto each end of one piece of chain. Finish the wrapped loops to join them to the chain securely. Repeat with two more beads on headpins and the other piece of chain.

4. Form a wrapped loop above the remaining two beads on headpins to turn them into bead dangles.

5. Open one earring wire and slip a link of the chain onto it—I chose a point just about ⅓ in. from the top of the chain. See how the two beads hang together and decide if you like their placement.

When you're happy with the arrangement, add one of the bead dangles from step 4 in front of the chain already on the earring wire and close it securely.

6. Repeat step 5 to make your second earring.

Pretty Curve Earrings

● ○ ○ **EASY**

This delicate teardrop curve suspends three semiprecious beads in a lovely configuration. I used small organically shaped red jasper rounds for my version, but you can substitute a single larger bead, a more perfectly symmetrical shape, or another semiprecious stone that catches your eye.

▼ **YOU'LL NEED**

Pliers

Six small semiprecious beads

24-gauge wire

Pair of earring wires

FINISHED SIZE

1½ in.

1. Cut two 5-in. pieces of wire and use your hands to form a gentle curve in each. Thread three beads onto each one and set one aside.

2. Bring both ends of the wire together and cross them above the beads, forming a compact, curved teardrop shape with an X above it. You'll use a modified version of the briolette wrapping method to create this piece. Use pliers to bend one wire at a neat, sharp angle where they cross, and wrap the other wire around it in a neat coil several times, ending at the back and clipping the wire there. (See "Briolette wrapping" on p. 25.)

3. Form a loop above the coil and wrap the wire end in a coil downward until it meets the first coil from step 2. Clip the wire neatly at the back.

4. Repeat steps 2 and 3 to make the second earring.

Family Birthstone Earrings

● ● ○ **INTERMEDIATE**

I came up with the idea for these earrings a long time ago, and by the time I found our four birthstones—and designed them—I was so happy to finally bring them to life. You can adapt this idea to use as many or as few birthstones as you like, and vary the sizes or cuts of your semiprecious beads to create the combination that works best together. You may choose to honor family members, friends, or perhaps a special anniversary month—this is a very personal design! The chart below right shows you which stones traditionally go with each month. You can see a matching Family Birthstone Pendant on p. 95 that uses similar beads with a very special locket.

▼ **YOU'LL NEED**

Pliers

Two drilled birthstone beads for each family member, friend, or anniversary you want to commemorate

24-gauge wire or the gauge that works with your semiprecious stones (I also used 26-gauge gold-filled wire for my emerald beads, which were drilled very narrowly)

Chain (I used only 1½ in. total for my compact earrings)

Pair of leverback earring wires

FINISHED SIZE

2 in.

1. Find the right birthstone beads for your design. I auditioned several different sizes and styles for some of mine,

but ended up choosing 4-mm garnets, 2-mm emeralds, 12-mm citrines, and 8-mm freshwater pearls.

2. Look at your birthstones and decide which ones look most beautiful together and which should be separated slightly in the design. I placed my garnet above my pearl and my tiny emerald above the more generous citrine.

3. Pass wire through each stone bead to make sure it is the correct gauge for wirework. I used 24-gauge gold-filled wire for my garnet and pearl and 26-gauge gold-filled wire for my emerald and citrine.

4. Cut 2-in. pieces of the correct gauge of wire, one for each bead or pairing you're using, and form a plain loop at the end of each one to create eyepins. (Note: The instructions from this point on refer to two bead dangles per earring, but simply adapt them to reflect your own design.)

5. Slip your beads onto each eyepin and form the first half of a wrapped loop above each one, without completing the loops. This will hold the bead dangles in place while you arrange them on the chain and finalize your design.

6. Cut two pieces of chain to the length you prefer (mine were ¾ in. long). Slip the link at one end of each chain into each of the leverback earring wires' loops. Close the earring loops securely.

7. Slip the smaller of the two bead dangles into a link of chain near the

top (I chose the third link of my chain) and the larger one at the bottom of the chain. Do not close the loops yet—just look at how they hang together before making a final decision.

8. When you're happy with the arrangement, complete the wraps to securely finish the earring.

9. Repeat steps 7 and 8 to finish the second earring the same way.

Birthstone chart

January	Garnet
February	Amethyst
March	Aquamarine
April	Diamond
May	Emerald
June	Pearl, Moonstone
July	Ruby
August	Peridot
September	Sapphire
October	Opal, Tourmaline
November	Topaz, Citrine
December	Turquoise, Zircon

My Favorite Earrings

▶ **TECHNIQUES:**

Wrapped Loops Treasure Jar Earrings, Pearls & Rings Earrings, Northern Lights Earrings /
Plain Loops Pearls & Rings Earrings / **Double-Wrapped Loops** Pearls & Rings Earrings /
Jump Rings Northern Lights Earrings

These three pairs of earrings are all very different from one another, but they all have that special, intangible quality that combines loveliness and fun. Each of them has interesting movement and a combination of very different elements, plus they simply make you happy when you're wearing them.

Treasure Jar Earrings

● ○ ○ **EASY**

I found an array of these tiny, perfect glass jars at Collage, a jewelry supply store in Portland, Oregon (see Resources on p. 184), and fell in love with their miniature scale. They offer endless possibilities for jewelry making. I filled mine with bright beads and suspended them from a simple wire loop. The Sparkle Jar Pendant filled with vintage sequins (p. 113) is a sister design.

▼ **YOU'LL NEED**

Pliers

Two small glass jars with cork tops and lips around the upper edge

Beads of your choice

24-gauge wire

Pair of earring wires

FINISHED SIZE

2 in.

1. Open both jars and fill them with something pretty, like beads, sequins, or something else tiny that fits through the neck of the jar. I like to fill mine about half full so there's some empty space at the top for contrast, but you can fill them to the brim.

2. Set aside two of the beads for later use. Replace the cork stoppers and press them securely into the jars.

3. Now you'll make a modified version of the double-wrapped loop to suspend the jars from earring wires. Cut two 5-in. pieces of 24-gauge wire and make a gentle rounded curve with your fingers about $1/3$ in. from the top of each piece.

4. Place one jar into the curve of one wire, so it falls within the narrowest part of the jar's neck, and create the bottom half of a wrapped loop, winding the short end of the wire around the longer to make a neat coil. Clip the wire at the back of the coil.

5. Thread one of the two beads you set aside earlier onto the wire spine and then form the top half of a wrapped loop above the bead. Clip the wire end at the back. Open an earring wire and slip the jar on facing front, then close the loop securely.

6. Repeat steps 3 and 4 to make the second earring.

Pearls & Rings Earrings

● ○ ○ **EASY**

My daughter's name is Pearl, and her namesake gemstone has always been one of my favorites. Pearls are serene and gorgeous, and they pair so well with other design elements like these simple, iconic silver rings. My great-grandmother's name was also Pearl, and I like to think that she would love earrings this pretty and timeless, too.

▼ **YOU'LL NEED**

Pliers

20-gauge or 24-gauge wire, depending on how your pearls are drilled

Two 9-mm pearl beads (I used a blush color)

Two ¾-in. metal rings (I used very simple three-dimensional sterling silver rings)

Pair of earring wires

FINISHED SIZE

2¼ in.

1. Cut two 3-in. pieces of wire that pass easily through the pearl beads, and form a plain loop at one end of each one. Place each pearl onto the wires, and form the first half of a large wrapped loop above each one (do not complete the wrap yet). Make sure the upper loop is large enough so that it can easily go around the ring and allow movement.

2. Slip the ring inside the first wrapped loop, then coil the wire to complete the wrap. Repeat to join the second pearl and second ring.

3. To connect the earring wire with the top of the ring, cut two 3-in. pieces of wire and create the first half of a double-wrapped loop with each one, making sure that the lower loop is large enough to easily go around the ring and allow movement, as you did in step 2.

4. Complete the wrap after the ring is inside the larger loop. Slip the earring wire into the top half of the double-wrapped loop.

5. Repeat steps 3 and 4 to finish the second earring.

Northern Lights
Earrings
by Lynzee Malsin

● ● ● **ADVANCED**

These beautiful earrings pair an organic curve of hammered metal with a crystal drop for a stunning design with plenty of movement. Use any bead or charm you like for this sophisticated piece. See the matching necklace on p. 68.

▼ **YOU'LL NEED**

Pliers

Hole-punch pliers

Hammer and hard surface (Lynzee suggests a mallet and steel bench block)

Sandpaper or a file

16-gauge brass wire

Marker

Four 4-mm jump rings

24-gauge wire

Two quartz crystal or other drops, drilled back to front

8 in. of chain

Pair of earring wires

FINISHED SIZE

4 in.

1. Measure and cut two 2-in. pieces of 16-gauge brass wire. File the wire with sandpaper or a file so that it's flat across the end and there are no sharp edges.

2. Gently bend each of the sanded wires into a V-shape. Set one wire aside.

3. Place the bent wire on a hammering surface (ideally a steel bench block).

Place the wire piece onto the smooth, hard surface and begin hammering gently to begin. You will quickly see how hard the wire is and how much force you will have to apply in order to get it to flatten and spread. Watch closely, as you will want to evenly spread and flatten the metal. Once you have hammered it to the desired flatness, mark a dot on each end with a marker to note where you will punch the hole for the jump ring.

4. Using the hole-punch pliers, pierce through each end of the hammered V, creating two new holes that you will use to attach the piece to the chain.

5. Using sandpaper or a file, sand the backs of the newly made holes to

prevent the piece from scratching your skin when worn.

6. Cut the chain into two 4-in. pieces. Set one piece of chain aside. Link the metal V to one piece of the chain using jump rings. Add an earring wire at the center of each chain segment.

7. Create a modified briolette wrap (see p. 25) to suspend the crystal from the V, overwrapping the coil with multiple layers of wire if you like, and slipping the top loop onto the V before completing the wrap.

8. Repeat steps 3–7 to create a second identical earring.

Vintage Gone Modern Earrings

▶ **TECHNIQUES: Jump Rings** Filigree Circles Earrings / **Gluing** Floral Post Earrings / **Double-Wrapped Loops** Vintage Button Earrings

I love to use vintage pieces in my modern jewelry, and these earrings are no exception. Each one takes a single fantastic element and lets it shine in a new setting. Whether it's a special filigree piece, cabochon, or button, each of these feminine designs starts simply and ends beautifully. ᡒ

Floral Post Earrings

🌷 🌷 🌷 **EASY**

If you're lucky enough to find a cute pair of vintage cabochons with flat backs, they make fabulous post earrings! Just make sure they're not too heavy to wear comfortably. These plastic flowers provide a ton of pop but not much weight—perfect for earrings.

▼ **YOU'LL NEED**

Two flat-backed cabochons
Two post earring backs
Strong glue

FINISHED SIZE

³⁄₄ **in.**

1. Make sure the surface you're gluing to is clean, flat, and dry. Place the cabochons facedown and apply a generous dab of strong glue to each one.

2. Press the post earring backs into each glued spot and let them dry undisturbed, checking after a few minutes to make sure that the posts are straight and even.

Filigree Circles Earrings

🌷 🌷 🌷 **EASY**

These pretty filigree designs are intricate without being fussy. Just choose filigree pieces you can pass a jump ring or earring wire through, and you'll be wearing them in a few minutes!

▼ **YOU'LL NEED**

Pliers
Two matching filigree pieces
Pair of earring wires
Two jump rings (optional, if you need them to connect the earrings to the wires)

FINISHED SIZE

1¹⁄₂ **in.**

1. Choose a place on the filigree design that you can wire onto with either a jump ring or the earring wire's loop. Open the loop or jump ring and pass it onto the filigree piece. Close it securely.

2. If you're using a jump ring, connect it to the earring wire.

3. Repeat to make the second earring.

Vintage Button Earrings

🌷 🌷 🌷 **EASY**

Here's another simple design that takes the charm of a vintage button and makes it very, very wearable. Use a sew-through button with two or four holes for this design.

▼ **YOU'LL NEED**

Pliers
24-gauge wire
Two sew-through vintage buttons
Pair of earring wires

FINISHED SIZE

1¹⁄₂ **in.**

1. Choose the side of the vintage buttons you'd like to use as the top of the earring, and which buttonhole you'd like to wire through for your design. For two-hole buttons, that can be directly above either hole. For four-hole buttons, it's usually easiest to arrange them so the holes are like a diamond shape with one hole at the top.

2. Create a double-wrapped loop, with the bottom half of the loop large enough to easily pass through the buttonhole, and complete the smaller top half of the loop to finish turning the button into a drop earring. Slip the button onto an earring wire and close securely.

3. Repeat step 2 to form the second earring.

Geometric Necklaces

▶ **TECHNIQUES:**

Bead Stringing Geometric Trio Necklace / **Jump Rings** Ovals & Circles Necklace, Triangle Duo Necklace

This set of necklaces is very open-ended, but the common thread connecting all three is the chance to use striking geometric beads and charms as an integral part of the design. Whether it's a row of ovals, a pair of generously layered triangles, or huge three-dimensional planed beads that instantly catch your eye, these necklaces are built around interesting shapes—and the negative space that defines them.

Geometric Trio Necklace

● ○ ○ **EASY**

This effortless necklace is perfect for a coffee date before work or an evening out. Three oversize wooden beads shaped with interesting planes and angles are suspended on a generous length of chain for a look that's as easy as it is stylish.

▼ **YOU'LL NEED**

Pliers

Three oversize wooden geometric beads (mine were painted bronze)

32-in.-long chain narrow enough to pass easily through the holes of the beads

Clasp or jump ring (see tip)

FINISHED SIZE

32 in.

1. Thread the three beads onto the chain and cut it to the length you prefer. Join the two ends of the chain with a sturdy jump ring if it's long enough, or add a clasp if it's not.

Tip: If the chain is long enough to pass over your head easily, you can simply join it with a sturdy jump ring instead of a clasp.

Ovals & Circles Necklace

● ○ ○ **EASY**

Another take on the geometric trio concept is this elegant row of gold ovals with tiny circles filling the negative space. I found these connector-style charms with loops on each side for easy joining, but you could also join open ovals or circles with larger jump rings.

▼ **YOU'LL NEED**

Pliers

Three oval or other charms in a striking shape (I used two that measured about 1 in. across and a central one that measured about 1½ in.)

Four jump rings

Chain of your choice

Clasp and ring plus small jump rings

FINISHED SIZE

20 in.

1. Join the three ovals with a jump ring between each one so they face forward. This will be the centerpiece of your necklace.

2. Cut two 8½-in. pieces of chain (or length of your choice) to flank the centerpiece. Connect each piece of chain to an outer oval using a jump ring.

3. Add a clasp and ring at the other ends of the chain.

Triangle Duo Necklace
by Cathy Zwicker

● ● ○ **INTERMEDIATE**

Combining geometric brass shapes with antiqued brass chain is a great way to create a unique statement necklace that can be both fancy and casual. This necklace can be modified to accommodate any sort of shapes, including chevrons, half circles, or rectangles.

▼ **YOU'LL NEED**

Wire cutters

Pliers

26 in. of chain (I used antiqued brass 2-mm rolo chain)

Two metal triangles with holes punched in two of the corners

Four jump rings

Clasp plus two jump rings

Hole-punch pliers (optional)

FINISHED SIZE

26 in.

1. Use wire cutters to cut the chain into two pieces that are each 2 in. long and two pieces that are each 11 in. long.

2. Use pliers to open one jump ring and loop it through the hole in one corner of the brass triangle that will be the lower piece of your necklace. Then link one of the 2-in. chain pieces onto this open jump ring. Close the jump ring securely. Repeat with another jump ring and the second 2-in. chain length on the other side of the same triangle.

3. Use pliers to open one jump ring and loop it through the hole in one corner of the second brass triangle. With that jump ring still open, loop the loose end of one of the 2-in. chain pieces that you just attached to the lower triangle piece. You will also loop the end of one of the 11-in. chain pieces onto this same jump ring. Close the jump ring securely with the pliers.

4. Repeat step 3 with the other triangle corner, the other 2-in. loose chain end, and the other 11-in. chain length. Make sure both sides are assembled the same so your necklace will hang correctly.

5. Add the clasp by opening a jump ring with the pliers. Use it to attach the clasp to the loose end of one of the 11-in. chain lengths. Complete the clasp by adding the last jump ring to the other loose 11-in. chain length.

Tip: I chose two different triangle sizes, but they can be the same if you'd like. If your triangles don't already have holes, you can add them using hole-punch pliers, as with the Northern Lights Earrings on p. 58.

Nature-Inspired Necklaces

▶ **TECHNIQUES:**

Bead Stringing Sea Glass Necklace / **Crimp Beads** Sea Glass Necklace /
Wrapped Loops Forest Park Necklace, Northern Lights Necklace /
Double-Wrapped Loops Forest Park Necklace

These necklaces are all inspired by color palettes found in nature: dreamy, watery sea glass; the spectacular northern lights; and the vivid greens in the forests here in western Oregon. Follow one of these paths or choose your own favorite range of colors found somewhere beautiful.

Sea Glass Necklace

 ● ○ ○ **EASY**

These smooth, dreamy colors were inspired by the Pacific Ocean. I mixed naturally shaped vintage costume pearl beads with faceted glass briolettes in the lightest, barely there aqua color. If you're using heavier beads, you may want to include fewer of them in your design. Just remember that an odd number of focal beads (three, five, or seven) creates a beautiful central pattern.

▼ YOU'LL NEED

Pliers

Seven glass briolette beads

38 freshwater or costume pearl beads

Seed beads

Soft Flex wire

Tape

Two crimp beads

Clasp (see p. 29 for instructions on making your own S-clasp)

Beading board (optional)

FINISHED SIZE

19 in.

1. Lay out your design in a symmetrical pattern, evenly spacing seven briolettes with two contrast pearl beads between each one. Arrange tiny seed beads between each of the larger beads throughout. Add 13 pearls on each side, each with a tiny seed bead in between, and end with pearls on each end of the necklace.

2. Cut a 24-in. piece of Soft Flex wire and then string the design onto the wire. Add tape to one end of the wire to hold the design in place.

3. Thread a crimp bead on the end of the wire that is not taped, add a clasp, and thread the wire back through the crimp and first few beads. Pull it taut and flatten the crimp bead, trimming the wire neatly.

4. Remove the tape and repeat on the second side to add the other half of the clasp.

Forest Park Necklace

● ● ○ **INTERMEDIATE**

My home of Portland, Oregon, has one of the largest city parks in the country, Forest Park, which generously stretches over a huge section of the northwest part of the city. It's beautiful for hiking, having picnics, or just taking a walk in beauty only minutes from traffic lights, houses, and shops. I love how green western Oregon is, and the color palette of this intricate bead centerpiece was inspired by the trees, ferns, and moss that thrive here so beautifully.

Design Principles: Botanicals

Flowers, leaves, trees, vines, branches, buds . . . these beautiful elements of the plants we see in nature, and in art and design, are endlessly inspiring. Whether you use specially made beads or charms to literally interpret botanical motifs, or suggest them in your overall design, the chance to include nature in your work is universally appealing. My nature-inspired collections found throughout the book often take their cues from botanicals.

▼ YOU'LL NEED

Pliers

18-gauge half-hard sterling silver wire for main necklace centerpiece

24-gauge sterling silver wire for charms

Craft wire for rough draft (optional)

One large glass oval, 1 in. wide

Two vintage Lucite cylinders, ³/₄ in. wide

Two faceted glass ovals, ³/₈ in. wide

10 smaller faceted beads

Two leaf charms measuring just over 1 in. long and 1¹/₂ in. long each

Chain of your choice

Clasp and ring, plus jump rings

FINISHED SIZE

19 in.

1. Turn the leaf charms into embellished drops by adding a small bead above within a double-wrapped loop for hanging. Make double-wrapped loops using 3-in. pieces of 24-gauge wire, placing a faceted smaller bead between the top and bottom half of your wire coil as a pretty embellishment. Make both charms the same way, so they hang facing forward.

2. Cut an 8-in. to 10-in. piece of craft wire to audition centerpiece designs and curve it into a gentle U-shape. (You can also use your sterling wire here if you like.) Place a piece of tape at one end to secure the wire, but you can easily add to either side to change the design.

3. Alternate each of the focal beads with smaller faceted beads (the same ones from the charm embellishments in step 1), using the largest bead in the center and flanking it with the two leaf charms on one side as an asymmetrical embellishment. Radiating out from there, add the medium-size beads and finally the smaller beads, always placing a small bead between the focal beads and charms, as you can see in the photo at left.

4. When you are happy with your design, transfer it to a curved piece of sterling silver 18-gauge wire 8 in. to 10 in. long, and form the first half of a wrapped loop at both ends, but do not complete the wrap yet.

5. Measure the centerpiece design at this point and decide how long you want your finished necklace to be. Mine measured 6 in., so I cut two pieces of chain, each 6¹/₂ in. long, to flank it for a finished length (with clasp) of about 19 in.

6. Slip the wrapped loop wire ends into the last link of each piece of chain. Complete the wraps to join them securely.

7. Add a clasp and ring at the other ends of the chain to finish the necklace.

Northern Lights Necklace by Lynzee Malsin

● ● ● **ADVANCED**

This elegant necklace matches the Northern Lights Earrings (see p. 58), offering a more generous take on the original smaller design. The longer hammered metal V centerpiece creates a beautiful, sophisticated line that draws the eye instantly.

▼ **YOU'LL NEED**

Pliers

Hole-punch pliers

Hammer and hard surface (Lynzee suggests a mallet and steel bench block)

Sandpaper or file

16-gauge brass wire

Marker

Two 4-mm jump rings

24-gauge wire

One quartz crystal or other drop, drilled back to front

20 in. of chain

Clasp plus two jump rings

FINISHED SIZE

24 in.

1. Measure and cut a 4-in. piece of 16-gauge brass wire. File the wire with sandpaper or a file so that it's flat across the end and there are no sharp edges.

2. Gently bend each of the sanded wires into a V-shape.

3. Place the bent wire on a hammering surface (ideally a steel bench block). Place the wire piece onto the smooth, hard surface and begin hammering gently to begin. You will quickly see how hard the wire is and how much force you will have to apply in order to get it to flatten and spread. Watch closely, as you will want to evenly spread and flatten the metal. Once you have hammered it to the desired flatness, mark a dot on each end with a marker to note where you will punch the hole for the jump ring.

4. Using the hole-punch pliers, pierce through each end of the hammered V, creating two new holes, which you will use to attach the piece to the chain.

5. Using sandpaper or a file, sand the backs of the newly made holes to prevent the piece from scratching your skin when worn.

6. Cut the chain into two 10-in. pieces. Link each side of the metal V to one half of the chain using jump rings. Add a clasp to each end of the chain.

7. Create a modified briolette wrap (see p. 25) to suspend the crystal from the V, overwrapping the coil if you like, and slipping the top loop onto the V before completing the wrap.

Semiprecious Necklaces

▶ **TECHNIQUES:**

Plain Loops Trio in a Row Necklace, Jade & Aventurine Links Necklace / **Jump Rings**
Trio in a Row Necklace / **Bead Stringing** Midcentury Turquoise Drops Necklace /
Crimp Beads Midcentury Turquoise Drops Necklace

Semiprecious stones—carnelian, jade, lapis, amethyst, citrine, pearls, and so many others—are some of the most beautiful beads you can find, and creating your dream jewelry designs with them is especially satisfying. The stones are so naturally beautiful that the simplest design and framing work to their best advantage, so here are a few ideas to bring your favorites to life.

Tip: Always check your semiprecious beads to see if the wire gauge you choose will fit through the holes easily. Some are drilled very narrowly, so you may have to use different beads or alter your design to use lighter-weight wire.

Trio in a Row Necklace

 ○ ○ **EASY**

A row of three round carnelian beads in graduated sizes is all this necklace needs to draw the eye. The natural color gradations and markings of the agates lend richness and luster to the simplicity of the materials. You can arrange them on a close-fitting curve or let them have a little movement, as I did, depending on your preference.

▼ YOU'LL NEED

Pliers

20-gauge wire

Three carnelian or other semi-precious beads, two smaller than the third

Chain

Clasp plus two jump rings

FINISHED SIZE

17 in.

1. Cut a piece of 20-gauge wire about 2 in. longer than the beads and curve it slightly with your fingertips. Make a flat-front plain loop (see p. 23) at one end and slide the three beads onto the wire in the order you prefer.

2. Decide whether you want the wire curve to fit the row of beads closely or leave some extra space for movement, and make a second plain loop at the appropriate spot. You can always move the finishing loop inward to tighten the design if you want to.

3. Decide how long you want your necklace to be and measure your center curve. My curve measured 1¼ in. across. I added 15 in. of length to that, so I cut two 7½-in. pieces of chain for the sides. Open one plain loop and slip the last link of chain onto it. Close the loop securely. Repeat on the other side to add the second piece of chain.

4. Use jump rings to attach the clasp to the other ends of the chain.

Jade & Aventurine Links Necklace

 ○ ○ **EASY**

I've collected a handful of jade, aventurine, and jasper beads in different sizes and all beautiful shades of green over the last few years and loved the idea of bringing them together into a simple necklace. Linking them with wire loops lets them all shine as a harmonious whole. This design would be lovely with identical semiprecious beads or with a lucky dip into your bead boxes to draw on a variety of colors or shapes.

YOU'LL NEED

Pliers

19 assorted semiprecious beads (I used jade, aventurine, and jasper ranging from ¼ in. to 1 in. across)

20-gauge wire

Clasp plus one jump ring

FINISHED SIZE

15 in.

1. Cut pieces of wire about 1 in. longer than the beads and form plain loops on both sides of each bead to make them into connectors. Don't worry about joining them yet; just make them individual and separate.

2. After you've added wire loops to each bead, begin arranging them into a necklace pattern. I chose a larger bead as my center and then did a fairly symmetrical pattern outward on each side, mirroring my bead placement side to side. When you're happy with your necklace, begin joining the bead connectors by carefully opening a plain loop, slipping another connector's loop into it, and then closing it securely.

3. When you finish the necklace, try it on for length. If you want to change the bead placement or overall length, it's easy to carefully take it apart and rearrange the order, or simply add more beads to the ends.

4. Add a clasp and ring to the ends the same way.

Midcentury Turquoise Drops Necklace

 ● ○ ○ EASY

I found an old secondhand turquoise and silver necklace that had seen better days and took it apart to give the pretty graduated turquoise drops some room to breathe. I chose to alternate them with wooden paddle drops and used the original sterling cylinder beads to space each one nicely. This necklace is simple to make but edgy when worn.

YOU'LL NEED

Pliers

Two 1¼-in.-long turquoise drops

Two ¾-in.-long turquoise drops

Two ½-in.-long turquoise drops

Five 1-in.-long wooden paddle drops, drilled side to side

26 sterling silver cylinders, ⅜ in. long

12 sterling silver cylinders, ¼ in. long

14 sterling silver rounds

Soft Flex wire

Scotch or washi tape

Two crimp beads

Clasp plus one jump ring

Beading board (optional)

FINISHED SIZE

18 in.

1. Arrange the turquoise and wooden drops in a repeating pattern to form the centerpiece of the necklace, placing the two longest turquoise beads in the center, flanked by the medium-length beads, and finally the shorter ones.

Place a wooden drop between each of the turquoise pieces.

2. Cut a 24-in. piece of Soft Flex wire and put a piece of doubled tape at one end. String the centerpiece design onto the Soft Flex wire, placing one sterling cylinder bead between each drop for spacing.

3. When you finish the centerpiece, begin adding more sterling silver beads on one side to build outward in a repeating design, alternating cylinders and rounds. Tape that end and open the other end to add sterling beads in the same pattern evenly on the other side.

4. Tape one end, then slip one crimp bead onto the open side and add the clasp there, passing the wire tail back through the first few beads and securely crimping the bead closed with flat-nose pliers before trimming the wire tail.

5. Repeat on the other side to attach the clasp's ring.

Holiday Party Necklaces

▶ **TECHNIQUES:**

Wrapped Loops Vintage Sparkles Necklace, Winter Pearls Necklace / **Jump Rings**
Sunset Necklace / **Painting** Sunset Necklace

Holiday parties are the perfect chance to make and wear something new and pretty. Who doesn't love a little sparkle? I made three very different designs for this mini-collection, and I love how fun they all are to wear. You'll find a few special pieces that coordinate with these in the Winter Pearls Hair Comb (see p. 125) and the Sparkle & Shine Bracelet (see p. 159).

Vintage Sparkles Necklace

  ADVANCED

Believe it or not, this pretty vintage necklace is made entirely from broken bits and pieces of old rhinestone jewelry. It started with two unmatched (and truly garish) 1980s rhinestone earrings and a loose flower piece I bought in a one-pound bag of broken jewelry years ago. I arranged them in an asymmetrical centerpiece, wired them together, and added sparkling crystal beads from an old opera-length crystal necklace of my great-great-aunt Sue's, which broke a decade ago. I just love the results and how sparkly and lovely it is when worn. It matches the Three-Generation Pendant I made for my mom (see p. 97) and the Sparkle & Shine Bracelet (see p. 159) beautifully.

▼ YOU'LL NEED

Pliers

24-gauge wire

Assorted rhinestone jewelry (I used two different earrings and a single flower setting)

Eight 7-mm crystal rounds

Eight 9-mm crystal bicones

Nine assorted smaller crystal beads for wiring the centerpiece sections together

Clasp plus one jump ring

Beading board

Digital camera

Craft wire (optional)

FINISHED SIZE

16 in.

1. Choose several broken rhinestone earrings or other jewelry to transform into a centerpiece and lay them out on a beading board. If you're using mismatched pieces, as I did, arrange them so they have a nice flow and balance without being strictly symmetrical. I placed a single broken flower element as my focal point and flanked it with the two earrings, adding a little pearl drop from one of the original earrings just to one side for fun. Once you're happy with your layout, take a photo for reference.

2. Turn the jewelry pieces over so the backs are facing up. Find places in the jewelry settings you can wire into or around to join them with beaded connectors. For a substantial necklace like this one, try to wire the pieces together with at least two connections each. I used a total of four connectors between my three centerpiece elements.

3. Cut four pieces of 24-gauge wire (or the number needed for connectors), each about 8 in. long. (For most wrapped loop-type connectors, 4 in. is enough, but 8 in. gives you more length for structural wire wrapping on one or both sides.)

(Continued)

Tip: I bought my rhinestone jewelry online more than 10 years ago, in a one-pound lot that I also used to embellish my wedding dress and veil, but you can find inexpensive rhinestone earrings and other jewelry in thrift stores, online, or in consignment shops.

4. Use the structure of your jewelry pieces as your guide to joining them. My flower piece had small holes ideal for wire wrapping a typical wrapped loop into on that side, while the earrings needed to be wrapped more creatively. Experiment with different spaces and techniques, using craft wire rather than more expensive sterling if you prefer. I recommend joining three pieces side by side with one connector between each, then adding a second stabilizing connector above or below it to finish. If your structural wire wrapping shows on the front, it will be subtle in the finished piece—just make sure it's sturdy and stable.

5. Add the first connectors as described in step 4, placing beads on the wire to space the jewelry out nicely before wrapping the second side. I used a total of eight beads here within four connectors.

6. When the necklace centerpiece works well, add a reinforcing second set of connectors near the first.

7. Cut two more 8-in. pieces of wire and wrap one end around the left side of your centerpiece, coiling the wire securely like a wrapped loop. Slip one crystal bead on the wire and add a wrapped loop on the other side. Repeat with the right side and another crystal bead.

8. Now add beads one by one, joining them before you complete the wrapped loops, to build a "chain" outward from both sides of the center. I used eight on each side, alternating between a round and a bicone bead. Add a clasp and ring to the bead connectors at both ends, joining them before you complete the wrapped loop when you reach the 16-in. length of the necklace.

9. Add a little embellishment to the centerpiece if you like. I added a pearl drop from one of the broken earrings to the right of my flower, with another crystal bead above it, just because it was pretty.

Winter Pearls Necklace

  ○ INTERMEDIATE

I used a curved branch decorated with little stems of "pearls"—a small section of a full-size floral spray from the craft store—to construct this necklace, and I loved the results. This would be beautiful with a more colorful, detailed silk-flower-and-leaves branch or even a few smaller and more delicate layers wired together.

▼ YOU'LL NEED

Pliers

One floral or decorative spray

24-gauge wire

Beads that complement your floral design (I used a total of six)

Chain

Clasp plus two jump rings

FINISHED SIZE

17 in.

1. Cut a section of floral spray around 4½ in. long to use for the necklace. You can go a little longer or shorter to capture special details within the branch, but this range makes a nice-size necklace center. Use your fingers to form it into a gentle curve.

2. Cut a 2-ft. length of 24-gauge wire. Leaving a 6-in. tail to work with later, begin wrapping the wire tightly around the left end of the branch, about four to six times total. Continue wrapping the wire across the branch to add stability, threading on a complementary bead and placing it on the front

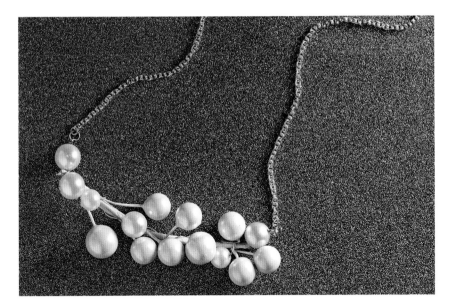

of the design to cover the bare wire about every other wrap. Depending on how lush or simple your branch is, feel free to add more beads to embellish the design. My costume pearl beads matched the original spray pretty closely, but contrasting colors, sparkle, or shapes would be beautiful, too.

3. Continue wrapping and wiring beads onto the branch until you reach the other end. Finish by wrapping the wire tightly four to six times. Thread one bead onto the wire tails on each end.

4. Make the first half of a wrapped loop above the bead on each of the wire tails. Slip the first link of a chain onto each of them, then complete each of the wrapped loops to securely hold the beads in place at either side of the necklace branch. Clip the wire tails at the back of each coil.

5. Trim the chain to the length you prefer—I cut mine to 5½ in. on each side—and add a clasp at the ends.

Tip: One floral spray is likely enough material to make several projects. For example, I made the Winter Pearls Necklace and matching hair comb (see p. 125) from a single long branch. Look for one with a sturdy stem and interesting details. If you find a more delicate stem, you could wire several layers together to "build" a sturdier necklace.

Sunset Necklace
by Torie Nguyen

  ● ● ○ **INTERMEDIATE**

Here's a fun and inexpensive way to dress up any outfit. You can also use your leftover materials to make coordinating earrings (see Sunset Earrings on p. 40).

▼ **YOU'LL NEED**

Three paint chips

1¼-in. circle paper punch

¹⁄₁₆-in. tiny hole punch

Gold spray paint

Washi tape or paper tape

Twenty 4-mm jump rings (you will use 15, but it's good to have a few extra)

16 in. to 18 in. of chain for necklace (or desired length)

Clasp plus two jump rings

Pliers

Ball-point pen or pencil

Dropcloth

FINISHED SIZE

22 in.

1. Choose which paint chip colors you'd like for each layer of the necklace. Use the 1¼-in. circle paper punch to punch out three circles for the top row, two circles for the middle row, and one circle for the bottom row.

2. Spread the dropcloth in a well-ventilated area. Lay the three circles for the top row in a straight line on the dropcloth, right sides up, so that they

(Continued)

are touching but not overlapping. Use washi tape or paper tape to mask off the area you do not want to spray-paint. Lining the circles up next to each other will help you mask them off evenly with one long piece of tape.

3. Repeat step 2 for the middle row of circles, masking less space on each row so the pieces become progressively more gold in each row.

4. Lay the bottom circle down, right side up. Paint the bottom circle entirely gold, or choose to mask some of it off—it's up to you!

5. Following the instructions on the spray-paint can, spray all of your circles evenly with one coat of paint and allow to dry. If you're happy with how that looks, continue on to step 6. If not, spray another coat of paint and allow to dry. Carefully remove the tape from the circles.

6. On a table or countertop, lay out the top row (three circles) in a straight line so the circles are touching but not overlapping. Where each circle touches another circle, make a small dot or indentation with a ball-point pen about $1/16$ in. in from the edge. This is where you will attach the circles together with jump rings.

7. Lay the middle two circles directly under the top row, centered. The circles should all be touching without overlapping. Use the ball-point pen to mark the point where the jump rings will go—about $1/16$ in. in from the edge of each place where the circles touch. Center the bottom circle underneath and repeat the marking process.

8. Use a tiny hole punch to punch the holes where you've made your pen marks. Make sure you are punching the holes far enough in from the edge so the circles don't rip.

9. Now it's time to attach the circles together using the jump rings, starting with the row of three. With pliers, open one jump ring, place the first circle on it, then add the second circle so that when the ring is closed, the circles will both lie flat with their right sides up. Close the jump ring securely. Repeat this process for each circle until they are all attached to one another, as shown in the photo above.

10. Mark the point where the jump rings will go to hang the necklace from the chain by using the ball-point pen to make a small dot or indentation at the 11 o'clock and 1 o'clock positions on each of the three top row circles. Punch out these marks with the $1/16$-in. hole punch.

11. Put one jump ring through each of these new holes and close them all securely. Thread the chain through each of these jump rings at the top of the piece. Attach one jump ring to one end of the chain. Use another jump ring to attach the clasp to the other end of the chain.

Tiered Necklaces

▶ **TECHNIQUES:**

Bead Stringing Midcentury Color Whirl Necklace, Deco Sparkle Necklace /
Wrapped Loops Modern Lucite Necklace

One of the most iconic vintage jewelry styles is the tiered
necklace—whether it's a timeless double strand of perfectly
matched pearls, a brightly colored mix of exuberant 1950s and
1960s Lucite beads, or a sparkly Art Deco–era cut-glass necklace a
flapper would have worn from a dance to a speakeasy. Creating your
own version in your favorite beads, colors, and style is easy when
you use a simple formula to ensure both tiers harmonize in length
and design. Reuse a vintage double clasp, find one new, or use a
simple modern trick to balance the tiers. No matter what clasp you
use, this necklace design comes together beautifully.

Midcentury Color Whirl Necklace

● ● ○ **INTERMEDIATE**

I love the beads, fabrics, and designs of the 1950s and 1960s, and I drew on that colorful era to make this aqua confection. Restringing a broken vintage necklace or mixing vintage and new beads in Lucite and glass are both easy ways to bring a design like this to life. I used a new clasp here, but you can see a few other options in the other two-tiered necklace projects.

▼ **YOU'LL NEED**

Pliers

60 assorted small, medium, and large beads in your preferred color or colors (I used a mix of Lucite and glass beads in shades of aqua)

Seed beads

Soft Flex wire

Small crimp beads

Double-stranded clasp

Beading board (optional)

Clear tape

FINISHED SIZE

20 in.

1. Start with the shorter tier (15 in. long) and build your design outward from a center bead (the shorter groove of a curved beading board will help with this). Plan to put a small seed bead in between each bead you place, creating a symmetrical mix of faceted Lucite, round pearls, and solid-color beads, and then add smaller ovals and unusual shapes as it grows outward. Try for a mix of colors, hues, and opaque and translucent elements. When the shorter tier reaches close to 15 in. in length, look over everything, make a few switches, if necessary, and then move on to the longer tier.

2. For the longer strand, lay out a 17½-in.-long design in a lower groove of the beading board. Add a smaller center bead (as described in Tiered Necklace Secrets on the facing page) and flank it with larger ones, reflecting the pattern of the first tier. Continue building the pattern outward, using some of the same beads from the first strand in different places and again mixing different hues and shapes to draw the eye. When the design reaches 17 in. long, take another look to see how the two tiers work together.

3. To string the necklace, start with the shorter tier. Cut a piece of Soft Flex wire about 22 in. long, put tape on one end, and begin stringing left to right, with a seed bead between each larger bead. Place tape at the open end when you are finished to hold the design. String the second tier the same way, using a 24-in. length of Soft Flex wire.

4. When both necklace sections are securely taped, hold them up together at each end to see how they hang as a unit. If you see any spots where beads push each other out of alignment, you can adjust the overall pattern to give them more breathing room and restring one tier until it flows nicely.

5. Remove the tape and place a small crimp bead onto the first end of the upper tier. Thread the wire end into one side of a double clasp and then back through the crimp bead and the first few beads. Flatten the crimp bead with pliers and trim the excess wire.

6. Repeat step 5 to add a crimp bead and finish the other end of the shorter tier. Do not pull the wire too tightly for this style of necklace—leave just a bit of space for the beads to lie fluidly and smoothly, not taut without movement. You want these beads to be able to curve to your neck nicely.

7. Repeat step 5 to attach the second, longer tier of your necklace to the other two clasp spots, again leaving a little space for the beads.

Tiered Necklace Secrets

Here are a few tips on designing your necklaces so the two strands fit together beautifully.

First, what size beads are you using throughout? Do they vary in size, or are they all the same? For the Midcentury Color Whirl Necklace (see the facing page), many of my beads were large, so I needed to leave space for the two strands to lie smoothly when I wore it. I planned a 2½-in. difference between the two lengths. After stringing my shorter strand, I placed it on a curved beading board so I could arrange the longer strand to follow its lead and fit nicely together. Bead stringing also offers an easy way to rework the order or change the design, unlike knotting or wire wrapping, which is more permanent.

You'll also see that in my Midcentury Color Whirl Necklace, the center beads of each strand nestle together nicely; the upper tier has a large bead, and the lower one has a small bead in the same center spot. This gives that large bead a little space to breathe, rather than cramming two large beads into the same exact spot on the necklace so they compete or push each other out of alignment.

The beads flanking them work well together, too. This time, the upper tier has smaller beads and the lower tier has large ones, so they also interact well when the necklace is worn. By the time I made the outer sections of both tiers, I was using all small and medium-size beads, which lie smoothly together, so I just focused on varying their color, shape, and translucence. Symmetrical, reflecting designs like these make it easy to mix in pretty details that harmonize together.

Plan Your Tiers!

If you're using all same-size beads, as in the Modern Lucite Necklace (see p. 81) and Deco Sparkle Necklace (see p. 80), it's much quicker to plan out your tier lengths. The beads of the Deco Sparkle Necklace were small and compact, so I only left an inch's difference between their lengths. The two strands can lie together closely without the beads touching or overlapping, and there's no need for symmetry or pattern within the stringing. For the Modern Lucite Necklace, I used an odd number of beads on each tier so that each one had a neatly placed center and then arranged them in their final layout via a chain on each side—you'll see more on that in that tutorial!

My last suggestion is that if you already have a vintage (or new) tiered necklace you like, look over its dimensions and details. Look at how the beads are organized in the overall design, or measure the tiers to find out how much they differ. You can learn a lot from a successful design, then make it your own with your color, bead, or clasp choices.

Deco Sparkle Necklace

● ○ ○ **EASY**

This ultra-simple necklace was inspired by its beautiful clasp—a vintage marvel with a concealed hook section and stunning details like cut-glass "jewels" set in its intricate sterling design.

▼ YOU'LL NEED

Pliers

120 sparkly or otherwise lovely beads (I used small faceted lavender/amethyst glass beads that measured six beads per inch)

Soft Flex wire

Four small crimp beads

Double clasp (I used a vintage one)

FINISHED SIZE

16½ in.

1. Choose the lengths for the two tiers of your necklace. Cut two pieces of Soft Flex wire 6 in. longer than the desired length of each strand. Since my beads were so small and symmetry wasn't crucial, I made mine 15½ in. and 16½ in., and I cut my Soft Flex wire to lengths of 21 in. and 22 in.

2. String the first tier and tape it at both ends to secure. Repeat to string the second tier.

3. Add a small crimp bead to each end and attach the necklace tiers to the clasp as described in the Midcentury Color Whirl Necklace (see p. 78). Again, leave a bit of space instead of pulling the wire taut so that the beads can flow together when you wear the necklace.

Modern Lucite Necklace

 ● ● ○ **INTERMEDIATE**

I think of this necklace as an understated, modern take on the classic double strand of pearls. I used clear oval Lucite beads for my version, but it would be beautiful in any monochromatic color. Wire wrapping instead of knotting provides a little more flexibility in the length and arrangement of the two tiers, and the adjustable chain sides make it wearable with different necklines.

▼ YOU'LL NEED

Pliers

20 beads of your choice (I used oval Lucite beads that measured just over ¹/₂ in. across)

Two smaller or coordinating beads

Seed beads

24-gauge wire

Medium or large-scale chain

Hook or lobster claw clasp

FINISHED SIZE

Adjustable

1. Begin wire wrapping the beads to build both tiers of this necklace the same way. Length is not as crucial on this design, as you'll see in a few steps—the beaded sections are centerpieces and don't need to fit your neck exactly. My beads were medium-size, so I planned a 2-in. difference between the shorter tier, which was about 10 in. long (9 beads) and the longer one, which was about 12 in. long (11 beads). Make each of the beads into double-looped bead connectors, with a seed bead on each side, joining them as you go to form two chains. I did use an odd number of beads in my design on both tiers so I had a center on each one.

2. When the bead chain approaches the approximate length of each tier, make sure you complete only *the first half* of the wrapped loop on the outer side of the two bead connectors on the ends. The two tiers should each have an open loop of wire on the outer bead, for a total of four.

3. Cut one 3-in. piece and one 5-in. piece of chain, one for each side of the necklace. Working with the shorter tier, slip the open loop of each end onto the first link of chain, with the 3-in. piece on one end and the 5-in. piece on the other end. Complete the wrapped loop to join them securely.

4. Now, slip the open loop on each end of the longer tier onto the chain, two links up from where you joined the shorter tier. *Do not complete the wrapped loop yet* but hold the necklace up to see how it hangs together. You may want to adjust the placement of the second tier, depending on the size of the beads, the number of links in the chain, or your personal preference. Move the second tier up or down the chain as you like, and then complete the wrapped loops to join them securely. I placed mine two links up from the first tier for a nice arrangement. Add the clasp to the 3-in. end of the necklace chain.

5. Make one of the complementary beads into a bead dangle and attach it to the end of the longer (5-in.) chain. Cut the chain about 1 in. above that point and make the other complementary bead into a double-looped bead connector. Slip the connector onto the links of the chain to rejoin it as a decorative element. Clasp the necklace anywhere along the chain's length to wear it longer or shorter.

Statement Necklaces

▶ **TECHNIQUES:**

Jump Rings All / **Painting** Chalkboard Necklace / **Gluing** Chalkboard Necklace, Floral Appliqué Statement Necklace

It seems like some pieces are just crying out to find the chain of their dreams and become a new heavy-rotation favorite necklace—the one you reach for first and plan your ensembles around. If you have a big, fantastical charm, appliqué, or piece of ephemera you've been saving for just the right project, maybe an ultra-simple but striking necklace is the way to go. You can also build your own statement using materials as varied as a tiny chalkboard or an intricate floral appliqué found in the bridal or formal section of a fabric store.

Octopus Necklace

● ○ ○ **EASY**

Choose just the right charm at your neighborhood bead store or in your stash. I thought this brass octopus would make a magnificent necklace. Pair the charm with chain that suits its style. I chose an elongated-link copper chain—I like mixing metals, and I thought the style of the two elements would work together nicely.

▼ **YOU'LL NEED**

Pliers

Large charm with holes or spaces on each side to link through (or you can drill or expand the holes yourself with a Dremel® or other handheld drill)

Chain of your choice

Four jump rings

Clasp plus one jump ring

Another necklace that you like the length of for easy comparison (optional)

FINISHED SIZE

17 in.

1. Using a measuring tape or another finished necklace you like for comparison, plan out the dimensions of your necklace. I knew I wanted mine to measure about 17 in. long, like another necklace I recently made that sits well. Since my charm measured 2½ in. across and my medium-size clasp and ring would take up about 1 in. total, I cut two lengths of chain, each measuring

almost 7 in. (Remember, it's much easier to make the necklace a bit longer and cut a few links off to make it shorter than to adjust it the opposite way.)

2. Use pliers to open one jump ring and join the first link in one length of chain to an opening on one side of the charm. (If need be, you can drill the holes yourself.) Close the jump ring securely. Join the other end of the chain to a clasp using a second jump ring.

3. Repeat step 2 with the second length of chain on the other side of the centerpiece and with the other half of the clasp.

Chalkboard Necklace

● ○ ○ **EASY**

This necklace is quite literally a "statement" piece—you can chalk or paint any message you like onto it! Use a small or medium-size chalkboard or framed piece for this lighthearted project.

▼ **YOU'LL NEED**

Pliers

Two jump rings

One small framed piece or chalkboard (mine measured 2 in. square)

Gold craft paint (or another color of your choice)

Paintbrush

Two 6-mm jump rings

Glue

Chain of your choice

Clasp plus two jump rings

Chalk or contrast paint with precision applicator (optional)

Tape

Chalkboard paint if your framed piece is blank (optional)

FINISHED SIZE

20 in.

1. Prepare the chalkboard. If the piece is blank, tape off the frame area and paint the center with one or two coats of chalkboard paint, letting it dry thoroughly between coats.

2. Remove the tape and paint the frame with craft paint and let that dry, taping the center off if need be.

Pliers

Hole-punch pliers or small awl

Floral appliqué (mine measured just over 6 in. across)

Heavy sew-in interfacing or Lacy's Stiff Stuff™, at least the size of your appliqué

Hand-sewing needle

Invisible thread

Scissors

Mod Podge® or other clear water-based sealant

Glitter

Paintbrush

Glue (I used Aleene's Jewel-It Embellishing Glue™)

Sequins and rhinestones for embellishing

16 in. of chain (or the length of your choice)

Two 4-mm jump rings

Clasp plus jump rings

FINISHED SIZE

22 in.

1. Place the floral appliqué over a piece of heavy interfacing or Lacy's Stiff Stuff and hand-stitch the appliqué over it, making small stitches and working your way around the perimeter. Knot securely when you have finished stitching.

2. Using sharp scissors, carefully trim away the excess backing and any negative space within the appliqué. Mix glitter into Mod Podge and use a paintbrush to apply it evenly all over the appliqué design. Let it dry completely.

3. Glue sequins, rhinestones, or other embellishments to the appliqué. I added a floral sequin and small round rhinestone to each of the flowers on my appliqué design, but you can add as many or as few as you'd like.

4. Use hole-punch pliers or an awl to carefully punch a small hole at each side of the appliqué design. Open the 4-mm jump rings and connect an 8-in. piece of chain to each side, passing the jump ring through the hole. Close securely. Add a clasp at the other ends of the chain.

3. Open each of the jump rings and pass them through the last link of an 8-in. piece of chain, closing them securely. Turn the chalkboard over and glue one jump ring at each of the upper corners. I glued mine at an angle, but you can place yours vertically if you prefer; it's up to you. Let it dry completely. Attach the clasp and ring to the ends of the chain.

4. If you'd like, use chalk or paint with a precision applicator to write a message on the chalkboard.

Floral Appliqué Statement Necklace

● ● ○ **INTERMEDIATE**

Choose a striking floral appliqué piece at a bridal or formal section of a fabric or craft store to make your necklace. You can embellish it any way you want, but I liked the simplicity of adding rhinestones and sequins to the center of each flower.

My Favorite Necklaces

▶ **TECHNIQUES:**

Bead Stitching Upon a Fold Necklace / **Jump Rings** Upon a Fold Necklace, Ladder of Pearls Necklace / **Wrapped Loops** Ladder of Pearls Necklace / **Knotting** Gold & Coral Necklace

These necklaces are all special in very different ways. Each of the three designers took a bit of inspiration from her childhood. Kayte Terry came up with a gorgeous fabric necklace inspired by folding origami, while Michelle Freedman created a pearl and chain confection like the special handmade necklaces she loved seeing her mother and grandmother wear. I reworked a classic graduated strand of pearls I remember as a little girl as the height of elegance in a bright gold and coral palette. I hope you're inspired to create your own take on a longtime favorite, too!

Upon a Fold Necklace by Kayte Terry

● ● ● **ADVANCED**

Using scraps left over from other sewing projects, this statement necklace high-lights the sophisticated beauty of origami-folded fabric. The addition of beads and sequins makes this showpiece an original work of art.

▼ YOU'LL NEED

Seven 4-in. by 4-in. scraps of fabric

Four 3-in. by 3-in. scraps of fabric

Iron (optional)

Sewing needle

Thread

Scissors

Two 8-mm jump rings

Pliers

Two 22-in. pieces of necklace chain

One 14-in. piece of necklace chain

Contrasting color thread and assorted beads/sequins (optional)

FINISHED SIZE

26 in.

Make an origami square out of each fabric square

1. Lay out one square in front of you, right side down. Fold it in half top to bottom, then left to right. Crease the fabric with your fingers. Unfold.

2. Using the fabric creases as guide-lines, fold two opposite corners of the square toward the center. Press with an iron (optional).

3. Thread a needle with sewing thread, make a knot at the end of the thread,

and stitch the two points of the square down to the middle. Don't worry about the back being a little messy, as it will be hidden.

4. Repeat steps 2 and 3 for the other two points of the square. You should now have a smaller square with all original corners folded to meet at the center.

5. Flip the square over so that the right side is facing up. Again, bring two opposite points of the square to the center and secure with the needle and thread.

6. Repeat for the other two points, and you should have a smaller square.

7. Flip the square over again. Bring two points of the square into the middle and secure with a needle and thread.

8. Repeat for the other two points to make a tiny square.

9. Repeat steps 1–8 to make six more squares from the 4-in. by 4-in. fabric and four more squares from the 3-in. by 3-in. fabric.

Make the necklace

10. Lay out the squares on a flat surface using the photo for reference. Use a needle and thread to carefully stitch the corners of each square to the square next to it to complete the pat-tern. Knot to secure, hiding the knots under the layers of fabric in the origami squares.

11. Use a needle and thread to stitch a jump ring to the center of the small square at the top right, and knot to secure. Repeat for the top left square.

12. Open the jump ring on the right side of the necklace with the pliers, slide the two lengths of 22-in. chain and the 14-in. chain onto the jump ring, and use the pliers to close the jump ring again. Repeat for the left side.

13. To add beads or sequins, lay the necklace out flat again and plan where you would like to embellish the origami squares. To add a bead or sequin, thread a needle and make a knot at the end of the thread. Sew each embellishment on individually, double knotting to the fabric to secure. You can use contrasting thread to add the embellishments, if you choose.

Gold & Coral Necklace

 **INTERMEDIATE**

This is such a simple and classic necklace design, but reinterpreting it in bright gold and vivid coral lends it a little something special. I made this necklace on my flights home from QuiltCon after a week packed with colorful inspiration and modern quilts—many of them interpretations of traditional designs, with that little something special that sets them apart. The coral silk beading cord sets off the shine and luster of the gold beads, and the unexpected pop of color gives the whole piece a very modern feel.

▼ **YOU'LL NEED**

Tweezers
Glue
Pliers
One card of silk beading cord (I used size 12) in bright coral
Two bead tips
Twenty-two 5-mm gold round beads
Twelve 8-mm gold round beads
Six 12-mm gold round beads
Four 14-mm gold round beads
One 16-mm gold round bead
Beading board (optional)
Clasp plus one jump ring

FINISHED SIZE

22 in.

1. Lay the graduated beads out on a beading board symmetrically, so they move from smallest at each end to largest in the middle in this order, left to right: eleven 5 mm, six 8 mm, three 12 mm, two 14 mm, the 16 mm in the center, two 14 mm, three 12 mm, six 8 mm, and eleven 5 mm. Your bead sizes may vary, of course, but this arrangement is very harmonious.

2. Unwind the silk beading cord from its card and stretch it out. Tie a single knot 2 in. from the end farthest from the needle. Add a bead tip to the strand so that the cupping halves face away from the needle and open toward the knot, then use tweezers to position a single knot just above the bead tip, pulling it taut.

3. Thread the 5-mm bead onto the cord and position it just above the knot. Now knot above the first bead.

4. Add more beads in the order you set them out on the beading board, moving around the necklace from smallest to largest and then back again. When you

add the last bead, make one more knot just above it to hold it in place.

5. Add the second bead tip onto the cord, so the cups are facing away from the beads. Tie a single knot inside the cups, again using the tweezers to position it neatly.

6. Cut the excess cord from the ends of the necklace, close to the bead-tip knots. Add a drop of glue to each knot to seal it, and then use flat-nose pliers to close the bead tips over the knots.

7. Add the clasp to one bead tip and curve it closed using round-nose pliers. Repeat, adding the ring to the other side the same way.

Tip: Beading cord is sold in different thicknesses. The smaller the number, the thinner the cord. My beads were drilled generously, so I used a 12—you'll want to make sure the cord can easily pass through each bead, but a single knot will stop it in its tracks so it can't slip over to bump its neighbor.

Ladder of Pearls Necklace by Michelle Freedman

 ● ● ○ **INTERMEDIATE**

My mother and grandmother often wore 14K gold pearl and chain necklaces that my dad made by hand for them. It was a source of great pride for me as a little girl that they wore—and loved—something that he had created. When I was a teenager, he made one for me. I couldn't believe that I owned something so beautiful and special. This is an updated version of those necklaces that you can personalize with your favorite beads and the number of tiers you choose to build. Use small, irregular freshwater pearls; find faceted, clear-tinted beads; and mix your metals to get this look.

▼ **YOU'LL NEED**

Pliers

24-k gold-filled wire

36-in. chain of your choice

Ten 4-mm jump rings

Nine ½-in. metal or glass bugle beads

Eight freshwater pearls

12 spacers

Three beads of your choice

Clasp plus one jump ring

FINISHED SIZE

21 in.

1. To make the tiers that hang across at the base of the necklace, cut a 4-in. piece of 24-k wire and form a wrapped loop at one end. String three bugle beads onto the wire. Create a second wrapped loop on the opposite end of the wire. Trim off any excess wire. Repeat to make two more tiers in the same fashion for a total of three tiers.

2. To create the bead links for the sides of the tiers, cut a 3-in. piece of 24-k wire and form a wrapped loop at one end. String a set of beads in the following order: spacer, pearl, spacer. Finish with a second wrapped loop. Repeat to make three more bead links in the same fashion for a total of four links. Connect each bead link to the tiers with a jump ring.

3. Cut two 3-in. lengths of chain. Attach a jump ring to the center (1½ in. from an end) and attach to the bottom of the tiers. For a variation, make them slightly offset so one end hangs longer than the other. Repeat on the other side.

4. Cut two 10½-in. lengths of chain. Attach to the jump rings of the top tiers.

5. To create two more unique bead links, start with a 3-in. piece of 24-k wire and form a wrapped loop at one end. String a set of beads in the following order to create a unit that is about 1 in. long: pearl, spacer, bead(s), spacer, pearl. Finish the link with a second wrapped loop. Make a second bead link in the same fashion. Remember that the beads can be different!

6. Cut the chain 1½ in. up from the top of the tiers on one side. Connect one of the wrapped-loop spacers with a jump ring. Attach the remaining piece of chain back to the spacer with a jump ring. Even out the length of chain to 10½ in. and trim off any excess.

7. Attach the clasp and ring to the ends of the chain. Create a dangle to hang off the ring with the remaining bead link. I added another 3-in. length of chain in the same fashion as I did to the bottom of the tiers for added drama.

Vintage Gone Modern Necklaces

▶ TECHNIQUES: **Plain Loops** Amber Floral Necklace / **Wrapped Loops** Black & Gold Floral Necklace, Amber Floral Necklace / **Double-Wrapped Loops** Black & Gold Floral Necklace / **Bead Stringing** Blue Floral Necklace / **Crimp Beads** Blue Floral Necklace / **Gluing** Blue Floral Necklace, Black & Gold Floral Necklace

All three of these pretty necklaces use intricate vintage floral pieces as the star of the show. Building a new necklace around something so special is a joy. I found the amber-colored Lucite brooch at a consignment store, and I found both the round floral pieces at Dava Bead & Trade in Portland, Oregon (see Resources on p. 184). No matter what kind of vintage flower element you start with, make it your own with special details and embellishments as you create your necklace. 🐿

Amber Floral Necklace

  INTERMEDIATE

Design this necklace around just the right vintage brooch. You can either carefully cut away the pin-back or leave it on, as I did.

▼ **YOU'LL NEED**

Pliers

20-gauge wire

One large floral brooch

Ten 8-mm faceted amber Lucite beads

Eleven 14-mm oval plastic orange beads (or beads that complement your brooch)

Clasp

Beading board (optional)

FINISHED SIZE

19 in.

1. Plan and lay out the design, using a beading board if you prefer. You can use all the same beads or alternate in a pattern.

2. Place the brooch facedown on the worksurface. Find a place to wire through or onto on each side of the brooch to turn it into a necklace.

3. Cut two 5-in. pieces of 20-gauge wire and form the first half of a wrapped loop at each end of both pieces.

4. Pass one of the wire loops through the first spot you chose on the back of the brooch, and connect it securely. Complete the wrapped loop when you are happy with its position. Slip a bead onto the wire and finish it with a plain (not wrapped) loop on the other side. Repeat step 4 on the other side of the brooch.

5. Cut 2-in. pieces of wire, one for each bead to add to the chain, and turn each bead into a connector with plain loops on each side.

6. Begin adding beads on each side of the brooch, carefully opening the plain loops to join them one by one and then closing them securely, following a symmetrical pattern, if you choose. Continue joining beads until the necklace is the length you prefer.

7. Add a clasp to the last loop on one side. Depending on the clasp style, it can hook right into the last loop on the opposite side, or you can add its ring there.

Tip: If there are any rough or sharp edges, you can glue soft felt over the entire pinback area to make it safe and comfortable to wear.

Black & Gold Floral Necklace

  INTERMEDIATE

I found this broken flower piece on the treasure table at Dava Bead & Trade in Portland, Oregon (see Resources on p. 184) and knew it would become something special. The piece features six flowers that curve around an identical center flower. I wired it onto the bead-and-circle components before gluing tiny rhinestones to the centers as a final fancy touch. Use your floral jewelry piece as inspiration to help choose beads and other elements to construct your necklace.

▼ **YOU'LL NEED**

Pliers

24-gauge wire

One vintage flower jewelry component

Four black faceted 9-mm beads

Four ¾-in. gold rings

10 in. of chain

Clasp plus two jump rings

Optional: Glue and rhinestones (I used seven tiny black ones)

FINISHED SIZE

18 in.

1. Choose two places to wire into to turn the floral piece into a necklace. I found spots at about the 10 o'clock and 2 o'clock positions. (See the tip below if your piece is a solid cabochon style.)

2. Cut two 4-in. pieces of 24-gauge wire and make the first half of a wrapped loop at one end of each, making sure the loop is big enough to pass through or wire around the spots you've chosen.

3. Slip the first loop through the filigree space and complete the wrapped loop on that side. Repeat with the other wire on the opposite side.

4. On the other end of the wire opposite the loop, make the first half of a double-wrapped loop, big enough so one of the gold rings can easily fit into the loop. Slip a gold ring into the second half of the loop and then complete the wrap to close the double-wrapped loop. Repeat on the other side of the flower. You should now have a gold ring attached to each side of the flower with a neat double-wrapped loop.

5. Cut four 4-in. pieces of wire. Set three aside for now. Form the first half of a wrapped loop at one end of the first piece, making sure the loop is big enough to fit around a gold ring. Slip the gold ring on the right side of the flower though the loop and then complete the wrap to join them.

6. Put one faceted bead on the wire and form the first half of a wrapped loop on the other side. Slip it into another gold ring to connect them, then complete the wrap.

7. Add another black bead to the gold ring, using a double-wrapped loop just as you did earlier. Leave the second half of the double-wrapped loop open for now. Repeat steps 5–7 to add rings and beads to the left side of the flower.

8. Cut two pieces of 5-in. chain. Join the outer beads' loops to the ends of the chain before closing the wrapped loops.

9. Add a clasp and ring at each end of the chain. **Optional:** Glue rhinestone centers or other embellishments to the flower piece.

Tip: My flower was a filigree style I could wire into, but if your flower piece is more of a flat-backed cabochon style without those openings, you can glue jump rings or pendant bails at either side, as in the Chalkboard Necklace (p. 83) instead.

Blue Floral Necklace

  EASY

This necklace is the easiest of the three versions to make. Just find a nice filigree-style base, add pretty things here and there, and string beads on either side to make a delicate necklace with lots of intriguing negative space to balance out the femininity of the design.

▼ YOU'LL NEED

Pliers

Filigree-style flower base

Assorted decorative elements (I used two flowers with flat backs, a rhinestone, and two vintage leaves)

Glue

120 4-mm faceted steel blue glass beads (or beads of your choice)

Soft Flex wire

Tape

Four crimp beads

Clasp plus one jump ring

FINISHED SIZE

19 in.

1. Choose some fun things to embellish your filigree flower. I glued two layered flowers down at the center, then added a small rhinestone. I also glued two angled leaves at about the 5 o'clock position on the flower. Let them dry completely after gluing.

2. Choose two spots to attach the necklace strands, as you did with the other two vintage flower necklaces (see pp. 90–91). I chose to add mine at about the 10 o'clock and 2 o'clock spots.

3. Cut two pieces of Soft Flex wire 14 in. each (or 6 in. longer than your desired necklace lengths on each side). Double a piece of tape at one end of each and set one aside.

4. String beads on the Soft Flex wire until you reach the desired length. Tape the other end of the beading wire to hold them in place. Repeat step 4 to bead the other side of the necklace the same length.

5. Remove the tape from one end of one bead strand and add a crimp bead there. Pass the wire end through the 10 o'clock spot on the flower (or where you want to add the necklace strand) and then back through the crimp bead and the first three or four beads. Crimp it flat with flat-nose pliers. Remove the tape from the opposite end, add a crimp bead, and join the clasp there the same way.

6. Repeat step 5 to add the beaded strand to the 2 o'clock spot and the clasp ring on the other side of the necklace. Trim all Soft Flex wire ends neatly.

Family Pendants

▶ **TECHNIQUES:**

Wrapped Loops All / **Plain Loops** Wedding Ring Pendant, Three-Generation Pendant / **Jump Rings** All

These designs are very personal, bringing special elements from your family to life. Whether you design something beautiful with your family's birthstones, incorporate a piece of heirloom jewelry like a wedding ring into your pendant, or include beads or charms passed down from relatives, this pendant will have a special resonance for you through the connections and love it represents.

Wedding Ring Pendant

● ● ○ **INTERMEDIATE**

A couple of months before my daughter, Pearl, was born, my wedding ring got too tight to wear comfortably. But I just couldn't stand the thought of not wearing it, since I love it so much—it was my grandmother's from her wedding in 1943, and it's very precious to me. So I made it into a little pendant with a single pearl dangling in the center. My ring is back on my finger now, but for this book I wanted to re-create this pretty project with a vintage sterling silver ring.

▼ **YOU'LL NEED**

Pliers

One ring

One center bead (I used a medium-size pearl, around 6 mm)

2-in. piece of 24-gauge wire

One headpin

Chain

Clasp plus two jump rings

FINISHED SIZE

17 in.

1. Slip the bead onto the headpin and form a wrapped loop above it to create a simple dangle. Clip the end of the headpin neatly.

2. Using the piece of wire, form a medium-size loop that will be the lower half of a double-wrapped loop (one lower loop catching the ring and one upper loop catching the chain, as you can see in the photo at right), but do not start wrapping the coil yet. Slip the

ring and then the bead dangle onto the open loop so that the bead hangs neatly inside the ring. Once those are in place, complete the wrap, winding the wire into a neat coil above the loop.

3. Form a second wrapped loop above the first one. Slip the chain into the open loop and complete the wrap. Finish the pendant by coiling the wire around two or three times, until it meets the first wrap in the middle of the coil. Clip both ends at the back. Use flat-nose pliers to flatten the edges.

4. Cut the chain to the desired length. Slip the pendant onto the chain, then add the clasp and rings to each end.

Family Birthstone Pendant

● ● ○ **INTERMEDIATE**

Like the Family Birthstone Earrings (see p. 54), this project is very personal and very customizable. I found pretty citrine, garnet, pearl, and emerald beads representing my family's four birth months and played with several different ideas. Ultimately, I chose to bead them symmetrically into a delicate chain around a vintage gold locket from my mother's side of the family for something of a Victorian feel. I tucked tiny locks of hair from each of my children inside my locket, but family photos or any other precious mementos would be lovely, too.

▼ **YOU'LL NEED**

Pliers

Two drilled birthstone beads for each family member, friend, or anniversary you want to commemorate

24-gauge wire or the gauge that works with your semiprecious stones (I also used some 26-gauge gold-filled wire for my emerald beads, which were drilled very narrowly)

Chain

Locket or other special pendant piece with jump rings for hanging it facing front

Clasp and ring plus two jump rings

Beading board (optional)

FINISHED SIZE

17 in.

(Continued)

4. Open one of the locket's jump rings and use it to connect the innermost bead chain loops. Hang the locket on this ring. If this makes the locket hang sideways, put the locket on a second jump ring and slip that onto the ring connecting the beads. Close all jump rings securely.

5. Measure the bead centerpiece to plan out the finished locket chain proportions. Mine measured 4 in., and I wanted my pendant chain to measure 17 in., so I cut two pieces of chain at 6½ in. each.

6. Slip the first link of the first piece of chain onto the partly completed wrapped loop from step 3 and complete the wrap to join them securely. Repeat for the second piece of chain on the other side.

7. Add a clasp and ring to finish the pendant. Fill the locket with something special. (I cut tiny locks of my children's hair and tied each one with a brightly colored strand of pearl cotton.)

Tip: *See the "Birthstone chart" on p. 54 if you'd like to design your own special birthstone pendant!*

1. Find the right birthstone beads for your design. I auditioned several different sizes and styles but ended up choosing 4-mm garnets, 2-mm emeralds, 9-mm citrines, and 8-mm freshwater pearls.

2. Arrange your birthstone beads in a row and consider which ones are prettiest next to each other or work better with a bit more spacing. I chose to place my dark red garnets, which were small but intensely colored, closest to my locket in the center, and put a larger, more serene stone (citrine) between my two most colorful, the garnets and emeralds. I originally started with the pearls closest to the locket, but since they were larger, they bumped one another above the centerpiece. This is a very personal process, and there's no wrong order—just keep moving beads around until you're happy with the design.

3. Cut a piece of wire at least 3 in. long for each bead and form each one into a connector with a wrapped loop on either side. Join the two sets of beads into two delicate chains in the order you chose in step 2. Do not complete the wrapped loop on the outermost bead yet. This one will connect with the chain ends.

Three-Generation Pendant

● ○ ○ **EASY**

My mother was very close to her great-aunt Sue and thought of her as a grandmother, and I know she misses her own mother every day, too. As the jewelry maker in the family, I inherited broken costume jewelry from both of them, and I used beads from these special pieces to make my aunts and my mother each a pair of three-generation earrings a few years ago. For this book, I wanted to make my mom a beautiful pendant using a sparkly faceted crystal bead of Sue's and a costume pearl of my grandmother's in a simple but gorgeous offset arrangement. No matter what scale or style of beads you use for this project, the chance to remember our grandmothers, aunts, or anyone we love best will make it especially beautiful.

▼ YOU'LL NEED

Pliers

24-gauge wire

Chain

Clasp and ring plus two jump rings

Jewelry display (optional)

Two or more special beads from family members (I used a 12-mm faceted crystal of my great-great aunt's and an 18-mm costume pearl of my grandmother's)

One 4-mm jump ring

FINISHED SIZE

18 in.

1. Choose the length of the chain you'd like to wear and cut it to that measurement, then add the clasp and ring at each end. Lay the finished chain flat or put it on the display if you're using one.

2. Choose a link in the center of the chain and mark it with a bent piece of scrap wire.

3. Cut two 3-in. pieces of wire and a piece of chain at least 1 in. long. I used exactly 1 in. of chain to suspend my two beads closely together, but you can certainly use longer chain for a more elongated design.

4. Form a plain loop at the end of both pieces of wire and place one of your special beads on each one. Form the first half of a wrapped loop above each one.

5. Slip the first bead dangle onto one end of the 1-in. piece of chain and complete the wrap to join them. Slip the second bead dangle onto the other end of the chain and complete that wrap, too.

6. Open the 4-mm jump ring and slip it through a link of chain closer to the smaller bead. I chose the fourth link of my chain up from the bead, but depending on your chain and beads, you might like different spacing. Move the jump ring until you like the way the beads are suspended together, and then carefully slip the jump ring into the link of the chain you marked in step 2 to join the dangle to the necklace. Close the jump ring securely.

7. Cut the chain to the desired length. Slip the pendant onto the chain, then add the clasp and rings to each end.

Design Principles: Somewhere for the Eye to Land

This is an idea I also love exploring in my modern quilting—giving your viewer's eye somewhere to rest in its overall appreciation of your work. This can be negative-space-driven or an element of your jewelry that just offers a calm or inviting effect. For example, my serene vintage gold locket is suspended on a chain with a row of glossy, beautiful birthstone beads. I could have looked for a more elaborate centerpiece, but the chance to include something understated lets those beads shine, even as supporting players.

Lucky Charm Pendants

▶ **TECHNIQUES: Jump Rings** All

I love making jewelry with the charms I've collected, and who couldn't use a little extra good luck in the bargain? These three pendants are a pretty way to spotlight lucky charms, from wishbones and horseshoes to a Bakelite four-leaf clover that's sure to keep your day's allotment of parking tickets and coffee spills to a minimum.

Horseshoe Pendant

● ○ ○ **EASY**

Horseshoes have long been seen as a lucky symbol, and they're always displayed with the ends facing up to hold the luck in. When I found this little vintage brass horseshoe, I thought it would be perfect on a delicate chain with the charm at the hollow of my throat. If you happen to find a larger-scale version, be sure to use a sturdier chain to make your pendant.

▼ **YOU'LL NEED**

Pliers

One horseshoe charm with the two ends drilled

Two jump rings for the charm

Chain

Clasp plus two jump rings

FINISHED SIZE

17 in.

1. Open the two jump rings and pass one through each of the holes on both sides of a horseshoe charm.

2. Cut two pieces of chain, one for each side of the charm. (Mine measured 8 in. each for a close-fitting but not tight necklace.) Slip one jump ring onto the last link of each of the pieces of chain and close the jump rings securely.

3. Add a clasp to the other end of the chains.

Double Luck Pendant

● ○ ○ **EASY**

Arranging two delicate charms as a pair so they clink together is a lovely way to wear them. I threaded an evil eye and a wishbone together on a longer chain for a pretty effect. Choose an unusual chain if you like for an intriguing part of the design.

▼ **YOU'LL NEED**

Pliers

Two lucky charms of your choice

Two jump rings for charms

Chain (my vintage chain with elongated links joined by jump rings measured 32 in.)

Clasp plus jump rings, or one jump ring (see step 2 below)

FINISHED SIZE

34 in.

1. Open the jump rings of each charm and slip them into the same link of the chain, as I did, or just onto the chain so they move freely. Close the jump rings securely.

2. Add a clasp and ring to the ends of the chain or, if it's long enough to easily slip over your head, join it with a jump ring.

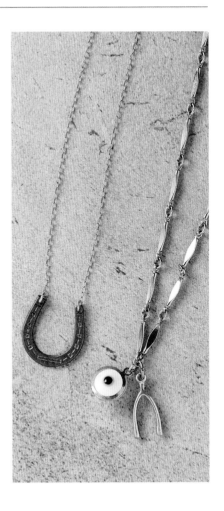

Lucky Button Pendant

● ○ ○ **EASY**

This Bakelite four-leaf clover button was a lucky find in a "poke box" at a vintage store, and I knew I'd use it for something special. Shank-style buttons (with a loop at the back instead of holes to sew through) are perfect to wear as a pendant on a metal neckwire—they slip on easily and sit beautifully at the center.

▼ **YOU'LL NEED**

Pliers

One shank-style button (like my cloverleaf)

Neckwire

FINISHED SIZE

16 in.

1. Slip the button onto a metal neckwire. Some neckwires have a round ball at one end that unscrews, while others (like mine) are sold with one end open to add the pendant.

2. Close the neckwire to secure the pendant. For a style like mine, use round-nose pliers to make a curve at the open end, so it will neatly close around the other side with its metal ball "hook."

Semiprecious Pendants

▶ **TECHNIQUES:**

Wrapped Loops Solo Perfection Pendant / **Plain Loop** Aventurine Dream
Pendant, Solo Perfection Pendant / **Briolette Wrapping** Coral Row Pendant /
Jump Rings All

For this collection of pendants, I wanted to use a few less
expected semiprecious stones, so instead of my instant favorites
(pearls, carnelian, and citrine), I found equally beautiful lemon
quartz, aventurine, and coral. Make these pendants to match your
Semiprecious Earrings (see p. 52) or Semiprecious Charm Bracelet
(see p. 149) exactly, or strike out on your own path to make
something unique and beautiful.

Solo Perfection Pendant

● ○ ○ **EASY**

For this ultra-simple piece, choose a single, special semiprecious bead or stone that's drilled vertically to hang as a pendant. I fell in love with this faceted piece of lemon quartz and its elegant, unexpected shape—not symmetrical, not square, just beautiful.

▼ **YOU'LL NEED**

Pliers

One semiprecious stone bead, drilled vertically with a hole wide enough for 20-gauge wire to pass through (I used a beautiful piece of lemon quartz about 1¼ in. tall)

20-gauge wire

Chain of your choice, sturdy enough to hold the weight of the pendant

FINISHED SIZE

16 in.

1. Cut a piece of wire about 4 in. longer than the bead, and make a small plain loop at one end.

2. Pass the stone onto the wire above the plain loop, and then form a wrapped loop above it, making the coil neat and close fitting. Clip at the back of the piece.

3. Put the pendant onto a chain and make sure it's sturdy enough to hold it.

Tip: Semiprecious stones of any appreciable size are often heavy, so make sure you use a heavier gauge of wire and a strong chain, and don't pile too much weight to wear comfortably. My lemon quartz pendant is a substantial piece, so I kept it very simple to avoid heaviness.

Aventurine Dream Pendant

● ○ ○ **EASY**

This simple elongated pendant suspends two rectangular beads of different lengths below a smaller round bead. I chose dreamy, cloudy aventurine for my necklace, but any semiprecious stone you love could work beautifully.

▼ **YOU'LL NEED**

Pliers

Two long rectangular beads of different lengths (I used one that was 1 in. long and one that was 1½ in. long)

One round bead

20-gauge wire

Three jump rings

Sturdy chain (mine was 30 in. long)

Clasp plus jump rings, or one jump ring

FINISHED SIZE

30 in.

1. Cut three wire lengths about 2 in. longer than each of the three beads and make them into bead connectors with plain loops on both sides of the bead.

2. Open a jump ring and slip the longer rectangular bead's plain loop onto it. Close it securely. Now, open a second jump ring and slip that ring and the plain loops of both the shorter rectangular bead and the round bead onto it, linking all three components. Close it securely.

3. Carefully open the round bead's other plain loop and slip it onto the chain. (I attached mine to a single link of chain to hold it in place, but you can also just put it on the chain to move freely.) Close it securely.

4. Add a clasp to each end of the chain or, if it's long enough to slip over your head easily, just join it with a jump ring.

Design Principles: Elongated vs. Compact

Instead of a predictable combination, consider suspending a small or delicate piece on a longer chain, or building a detailed or elaborate necklace that fits closely. What effect are you drawn to when you look at a special charm or oversize beads? Use that vision or idea in your design just for them.

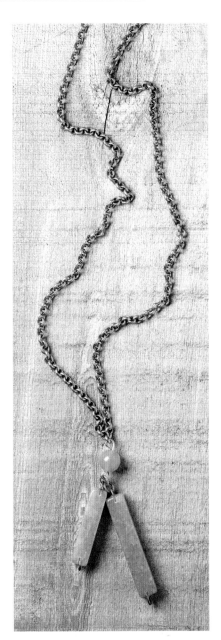

Coral Row Pendant

● ○ ○ **EASY**

This simple "hanger" style is an easy way to display a row of horizontally drilled semiprecious beads—in this case, natural, organic shapes of imitation coral. The sterling hanger allows plenty of movement while keeping the beads organized in an appealing line. Change the scale to use more delicate or heavier semiprecious beads of your choice.

▼ **YOU'LL NEED**

Pliers

20-gauge sterling or gold-filled wire (or the correct gauge for your beads)

Five organically shaped pieces of imitation coral that range from ¹/₂ in. to ³/₄ in. long (or horizontally drilled beads of your choice)

Craft wire (optional)

Chain

Clasp and ring plus two jump rings

FINISHED SIZE

18 in.

1. Arrange the beads from side to side in the order you prefer and measure them. My five elongated pieces of coral measured ³/₄ in. across lying next to each other.

2. Cut a piece of 20-gauge wire at least 4 in. longer than the measurement you took in step 1. The extra 4 in. will make a relatively closely shaped hanger like mine, while you can have more flexibility and difference of bead sizes with a longer piece. Experiment with craft wire if you like before cutting your sterling or gold-filled wire.

3. Make a sharp 90-degree-angle bend with flat-nose pliers in the wire about one-third of the way across. Slide the beads onto the wire and push them against the bend so they are flush with the wire angle. Now make a second bend at the other end of the row of beads, leaving a small amount of space for bead movement, the same way. The beads should now be neatly suspended in a horizontal row between two vertical walls of wire.

4. Continue making the hanger as a modified version of the briolette wrapping technique by bending the two wire ends so they cross each other like an ✕.

5. Use the pliers to bend the longer wire at a neat, sharp angle where the two wires cross, and wrap the other (shorter) wire around it in a neat coil several times, ending at the back and clipping the wire there. (See "Briolette wrapping" on p. 25.)

6. Slip the hanger onto the chain. Add a clasp at one end and a ring at the other.

Nature-Inspired Pendants

▶ **TECHNIQUES:**

Jump Rings All / **Crimp Beads** Feather & Circle Pendant / **Wrapped Loops** Filigree Leaves Pendant / **Painting** Framed Floral Pendant / **Gluing** Framed Floral Pendant

For this set of pendants, I drew on a wider mix of natural charms, motifs, and materials to create three very different designs. The simple pairing of a feather and a vintage stamped metal circle, the contrast of two very different metal leaf charms, and the intricate little flower-and-leaves design neatly spotlighted within a frame are all inviting, spare, and very wearable.

Feather & Circle Pendant

● ○ ○ **EASY**

Like the Double Luck Pendant (see p. 99), this pendant pairs two charms and lets them swing and move together. I've had this stamped metal circle charm for years, and when I found the intricate little feather recently, I thought they looked pretty as a pair. Wearing them on a colorful little ribbon instead of a chain adds a feminine touch.

▼ **YOU'LL NEED**

Pliers

Two charms of different sizes— a smaller one and a larger background piece

One jump ring

¼-in.-wide satin ribbon (mine was 24 in. long)

Scissors

Two large crimp beads

Clasp

FINISHED SIZE

16 in.

1. Open the jump ring and put both charms on it so that one hangs in front of the other. Close it securely.

2. Trim the ribbon's ends at a sharp diagonal angle so that you will be able to thread them through the crimp beads easily. Slip the pendant ring onto the ribbon and center it. Slip one crimp bead onto each end of the ribbon, pushing it down a few inches.

3. Add the clasp on one side, and then double the ribbon back through the crimp bead, catching the clasp in the loop of ribbon. Make sure the ribbon isn't twisted but is lying smooth and flat.

4. Repeat step 3 to add the clasp to the other side of the ribbon. Make sure that the pendant ribbon is the right length and make any other adjustments you'd like.

5. Use flat-nose pliers to crimp both beads securely, then trim the excess ribbon tails with scissors.

Filigree Leaves Pendant

 ● ● ○ **INTERMEDIATE**

I love to make jewelry "cousins," and this pendant was a fun project to design as a set with a few favorites from other parts of the book. It mixes leftover pieces from both my Filigree Leaves Earrings (see p. 47) and Forest Park Necklace (see pp. 66–67). A smooth brass leaf is balanced with a more delicate filigree style on an understated chain that lets them both shine.

▼ YOU'LL NEED

Pliers

20-gauge wire (use a lighter gauge for more delicate pieces)

Two different leaf or other natural shape charms, both drilled back to front

Two beads that complement the leaf charms

One 4-mm jump ring

Chain of your choice

Clasp with ring plus two jump rings

Jewelry display (optional)

FINISHED SIZE

24 in.

1. Cut the chain to the desired length and add a clasp at one end and a ring at the other. Place it on a jewelry display or lay it flat. Mark the center link by slipping a piece of scrap wire into it.

2. Cut two 4-in. pieces of wire and form the first half of a generously sized wrapped loop at one end of each. Slip one leaf charm into each open loop, then complete the wrap to secure the charms.

3. Slip a bead onto each wire above the coil. Form the first half of a wrapped loop above each bead but do not complete the wrap yet.

4. Place the larger or more opaque of the two charm dangles at the center of the chain you marked in step 1. Slip the charm's open loop into the link of chain.

5. Decide where the smaller or more delicate leaf charm should go in relation to the first one. I liked mine suspended above the first one, so I marked the spot one link above the first charm on each side of the chain and linked them with the 4-mm jump ring, closing it securely. Then I slipped the open loop of the second leaf charm into that jump ring.

6. Look at or try on the pendant to see how you like the leaves together. When you are happy with the design, complete the wrapped loops on both charm dangles.

Framed Floral Pendant

● ● ○ **INTERMEDIATE**

I have always loved simple designs, and the well-balanced floral and botanical textiles of the Wiener Werkstätte collective (c. 1910) are endlessly appealing to me. The little "flower" on my pendant was inspired by those clever lines and shapes, while both the color palette and the leaves extending past the frame keep it very bright and modern. Look for interesting marquise and round rhinestones to play with for your focal design, as well as glass squares that fit neatly into a metal frame with a pendant loop as the backdrop.

▼ YOU'LL NEED

Pliers

One 1-in. light blue glass square

Glass paint and paintbrush

One 18-mm golden yellow round flat-backed rhinestone

Two ½-in.-long kelly green marquise-shaped flat-backed rhinestones

Strong glue

Pendant frame that fits your glass square (see tip at right for an alternative way to finish your piece without a frame)

Chain

Clasp and ring plus two jump rings

FINISHED SIZE

18 in.

1. Apply two coats of glass paint to the back of the glass square, letting them dry completely between coats.

2. Glue the square securely into the pendant frame. Let it dry completely.

3. Arrange the large round rhinestone just to the left and above the center of the square, as shown on my pendant (or in the design of your choice). Place two marquise "leaves" to the right and below the round, so that they extend off the glass, if necessary. The rhinestones may not stay exactly in place on the slippery glass, so you can use tiny pieces of doubled tape under them if need be. Decide on the final layout and take a photo.

4. Lift the round rhinestone, remove the tape if using, and secure it in place with a dab of glue. Do the same for each of the marquise rhinestones, pressing them down securely where they touch the glass.

5. Let the entire design dry before moving the pendant. Meanwhile, create the chain by adding a clasp and ring to each end. Slip the pendant onto the chain.

Tip: I found both my glass square and pendant frame at Collage in Portland, Oregon (see Resources on p. 184), but you can also finish the glass piece without a frame. (See Washi Tape Triangles Pendant on p. 110 for details.)

Geometric Pendants

▶ **TECHNIQUES:**

Jump Rings Trio of Circles Pendant **/ Gluing** Washi Tape Triangles
Pendant, Covered-Button Pendant

Like the Geometric Necklaces (see pp. 62–64), this collection of
pendants includes strong, angular shapes and lines that use
geometry to define their focal points, along with plenty of negative
space to set them off. All three of these pendants are simple to
make, and all are just as effortlessly eye-catching.

Trio of Circles Pendant

 ○ ○ **EASY**

In perhaps the quickest project to make in the entire book, I've simply threaded three spare metal circles onto a chain and let them interact together with no setting, wiring, or beading. Use materials that work well together. Since my circles are lightweight, my chain is delicate, but for heavier or solid charms, be sure to use a sturdier chain that can hold them securely.

▼ **YOU'LL NEED**

Pliers

Three lightweight metal circle charms (mine measured about 1 in. across)

Chain

Clasp and ring plus two jump rings

FINISHED SIZE

19 in.

1. Thread three loose metal circles onto a chain and hold it up by both ends to make sure that it's substantial enough to carry the weight.

2. Cut the chain to the desired length—mine was 19 in.—and add a clasp and ring using jump rings.

Washi Tape Triangles Pendant

  ○ **INTERMEDIATE**

I found a super-fun triangle washi tape design to use for my pendant, but any strong geometric pattern would be great for this simple project. Decorative paper or photographs would work well, too.

▼ **YOU'LL NEED**

Pliers

One 1-in. glass square or 1-in. by 2-in. glass rectangle

Washi tape, decorative paper, or other interesting colorful background

JudiKins Diamond Glaze or other glass/paper glue

Strong glue

Acid-free cardstock

Pencil

Scissors

Pendant bail

Felt

Chain

Clasp and ring plus two jump rings

FINISHED SIZE

16 in.

1. Trace the glass square or rectangle onto acid-free cardstock with pencil. Apply strips of washi tape over the traced shape, lining them up neatly so the edges are harmonious. (Note: If you use decorative paper or another image, trace the glass piece over it the same way you did on the cardstock, capturing any details you like best, and cut it out. Glue it onto the cardstock.)

2. Cut the cardstock shape out and trim away any edges that show around the glass piece. Glue that to the back of the glass shape using diamond glaze. Let it dry completely.

3. Meanwhile, create the chain by adding a clasp and ring to each end.

4. Trace the pendant shape on felt and cut it out. Glue the pendant bail in place, at the center of the top edge, and then glue the felt backing over both layers. Let dry completely.

5. Slip the pendant onto the chain.

Covered-Button Pendant

 ● ● ○ **INTERMEDIATE**

This ultra-customizable design takes your favorite fabric patterns and translates them into jewelry quickly and easily. A single covered button is a striking pendant, framing and spotlighting a pretty print in a perfect circle. The Button Box Bracelet (see p. 156) is another way to wear your favorite fabric (or fabrics!), and the Covered-Button Barrettes (see p. 129) would be fun to match to your pendant.

▼ YOU'LL NEED

Pliers

One covered-button kit (I used both a ³/₄-in. and 1¹/₈-in. button for my pendants)

Small piece of fabric of your choice—I recommend a non-directional or multidirectional print, with details small enough so you can capture them within the button's face

Scissors

Glue

Plain sew-through-style button that fits behind the covered button

Pendant bail

Chain

Clasp

FINISHED SIZE

Length: 16 in.

1. Use pliers to remove the shank from the button backing. Following the covered-button kit package directions and template, cut out a fabric circle for the buttons.

2. Create one covered button, following the package directions.

3. Apply a generous dab of glue right into the back of the covered button and press the plain sew-through button into it. Let it set until the glue is mostly or completely dry and the inner button does not easily move.

4. Once the glue is set, use another generous dab of glue to attach the covered button to the pendant bail. Let the glue set completely before wearing. Slip it onto a chain or ribbon and add a clasp.

Tip: Covered-button kits generally come with five or six buttons, so you can make several pendants with one kit.

Tip: Do not use cute, inspirational buttons for the sew-through buttons—these behind-the-scenes buttons should be workhorses, not ballerinas.

My Favorite Pendants

▶ **TECHNIQUES:**

Wrapped Loop Sparkle Jar Pendant, My Favorite Tassel Pendant /
Jump Rings My Favorite Tassel Pendant / **Cross-Stitching** Cross-Stitch Pendant /
Gluing Cross-Stitch Pendant

This is (of course!) a very personal set of projects, reflecting
exactly the kind of jewelry you love best and what you most
like to wear. I love the tiny glass jars I found recently—they're perfect
for making beautiful, unexpected jewelry pieces to wear—and
filled mine with vintage sequins in an aqua palette. My kids (ages
six and four) inspired my cross-stitch initials pendants made just for
them. And Christina Batch-Lee came up with an ingenious re-use
for a vintage stamped brass finding rescued from an old necklace,
transforming it into an instant favorite pendant!

Sparkle Jar Pendant

● ○ ○ **EASY**

Like the Treasure Jar Earrings (see p. 56), this pretty pendant is just so much fun to wear. The intriguing, shiny contents shift and sparkle as the jar moves, drawing the eye in a pleasing way.

▼ **YOU'LL NEED**

Pliers

One small glass jar with cork top and lip around the upper edge (mine measured 1¼ in. tall)

Beads, sequins, or other small findings of your choice

20-gauge wire

Chain with clasp

FINISHED SIZE

19 in.

1. Open the jar and fill it with something pretty like beads, sequins, or something else tiny that fits through the neck of the jar. I like to fill mine about half full so there's some empty space at the top for contrast, but you can fill it to the brim. Replace the cork stopper and press it in securely.

2. Now you'll make a modified version of the double-wrapped loop (see p. 26) to suspend the jar from a chain. Cut a 5-in. piece of 20-gauge wire and make a gentle rounded curve with your fingers at about the one-third mark of the length.

3. Place the jar into the curve of the wire, so it falls within the narrowest part of the jar's neck (between the lip above and the wider section below), and create the bottom half of a wrapped loop, winding the short end of the wire around the longer to make a neat coil. Clip the wire at the back of the coil.

4. Form the top half of a wrapped loop above that coil, making the upper loop large enough to move freely along the chain. Clip the wire end at the back. Slip it onto the chain and add a clasp at the ends.

Cross-Stitch Pendant

● ● ○ **INTERMEDIATE**

I loved cross-stitching as a child, and I recently found these wonderful little wooden blanks with predrilled holes for stitching at Collage in Portland, Oregon (see Resources on p. 184). They're not only some of my favorite pendants to make, but they're my kids' favorites, too—they love the initials I stitched for them in their favorite colors.

▼ YOU'LL NEED

Wooden blank with predrilled holes (I used a round one and a flower-shaped one that measured about 1½ in. across)

Pencil

Two or more colors of pearl cotton or embroidery floss

Needle

Pendant bail

Felt

Scissors

Pliers

Glue

Thin leather cord in a coordinating color (mine measured 16 in. for a child's pendant)

Two small crimp ends

Clasp and ring plus two jump rings

FINISHED SIZE

16 in.

1. Thread the needle with the background color of floss or cotton. I used a single strand of pearl cotton for my stitching.

2. Fill in the outer rim of the stitching area with cross-stitch ✕s, moving

clockwise around the wooden blank. There are many good cross-stitch tutorials and books that can offer detailed instructions, but see the instructions on p. 32 to get started.

3. Continue stitching ✕s around the perimeter of the wooden blank, catching the thread tail inside the back of your stitching for security. For larger wooden blanks like mine, stitch two full rows of the design in background thread. If you're using a smaller one (say, 1 in. wide), stop at one row. When you've finished, guide the needle through a row of stitching on the back of the blank and pull it through so that the thread is caught in place like a knot.

4. Use a pencil to lightly trace an initial or other shape onto the front of the blank, framed by the background stitching. You can also find beautiful

cross-stitch alphabets online or in books, or you can draw them out on graph paper.

5. Thread the needle with the second color and create your initial, working from the outside in. If you don't like the way it's coming together, unpick it by reversing your stitches with the needle, or take the needle off and gently tug the thread back out to start again. This is a very personal project, so think about the recipient and what letter style he or she might like.

6. Once you're happy with the letter itself, guide the needle through the back of your stitching as you did in step 3 to knot it. Rethread the needle with the background color and fill in the rest of the space around the letters with ✕s. Secure the thread tail when you're finished.

7. Glue a pendant bail at the top center on the back of the wooden blank. Trim the felt to just smaller than the wooden blank. Glue it down over the entire stitching area and pendant bail. Let it dry completely. Slip the pendant onto the cord and check the length. Trim the leather to your preferred length.

8. Slip a crimp end onto one end of the cord, hold it in place, and firmly crimp it closed with flat-nose pliers. There are several different types of crimp ends, so make sure you follow the specific directions that work with yours.

9. Repeat Step 8 on the other side with the other crimp end. Add a clasp and ring with small jump rings.

My Favorite Tassel Pendant by Christina Batch-Lee

● ● ○ **INTERMEDIATE**

The top of this favorite piece features a stamped brass vintage finding that was originally meant to hold multiple strands of a necklace (one at each side of the neck).

▼ **YOU'LL NEED**

Vintage finding for pendant

Chain for necklace of desired length (I used 5-mm-wide vintage brass rope chain)

Chain for tassel (15 in. of 3-mm flat curb chain)

Two 4-mm faceted amethyst gemstone beads (or beads of your choice for accent)

One 3-mm jump ring

Two 6-mm jump rings

One 8-mm jump ring

One 10-mm jump ring

Two flat-head pins

Pliers

Lobster claw clasp

FINISHED SIZE

30 in.

1. To create the pendant, start with the tassel: Cut the 3-mm curb chain into six equal lengths, measuring approximately 2½ in. each. Open one 6-mm jump ring and slip one end of each chain length onto the ring. Close the jump ring. Use the 3-mm jump ring to connect the finished tassel to the bottom of the pendant.

2. Add each gemstone bead to a flat-head pin. Make a wrapped loop at the top of each pin; snip excess wire with cutters. Attach the finished loops to both sides of the pendant.

3. Add a large (10-mm) jump ring to attach the pendant to the necklace chain.

4. Measure the chain to the desired length for the necklace. Add the lobster claw clasp to one end of the chain with the other 6-mm jump ring and add the 8-mm jump ring to the other end of the chain to catch the clasp.

Tip: If you find two identical vintage findings, you could make a stunning pair of earrings instead of a necklace by repeating the steps for the pendant and attaching both to ear wires.

Tip: If you're making this necklace as a gift, add an extension chain at the clasp so the length can be customized. Add 2 in. to 3 in. of an open link chain opposite the clasp. Be sure the links are large enough to catch the clasp. Add a decorative bead or gem at the end of the extension chain, just for a pretty finish.

Vintage Gone Modern Pendants

▶ TECHNIQUES: **Wrapped Loop** Vintage Glamour Pendant / **Jump Rings** All

Tip: Look through all three of these projects for adapting and setting your clip earrings into pendants before starting this project. Each one uses a different technique, and one may suit your particular vintage earring piece best.

For this set of pendants, I chose a common vintage jewelry piece we all see at estate sales, thrift stores, and rummage sales—clip earrings! Nearly everyone who wears earrings has their ears pierced now, but half a century ago, that wasn't the case. I love to find colorful or striking clip earrings and rework some of their components into new jewelry using jump rings, wire wrapping, or a combination of techniques. These three pieces couldn't be more different, but I love how each of them found new life in a pendant setting instead of languishing at the bottom of a jewelry box. ᎒

Ring of Flowers Pendant

 **EASY**

This necklace was made from the dangling section of an old pair of earrings: a Lucite ring of pretty pink flowers set with sparkly rhinestone centers, which was crying out to be worn and loved again. I simply took the whole section off its clip and used jump rings to anchor a chain to the back of this pretty design, so it appeared to float in front of the chain.

▼ **YOU'LL NEED**

Pliers

One clip earring with dangle

Jump rings

16-in.-long chain (I recommend a medium-weight chain with links large enough to easily pass a jump ring through, not a very delicate or oversize style)

Clasp and ring

FINISHED SIZE

16 in.

1. Turn the earring over and look for two or more places you can attach it directly to a chain with jump rings. Since my earring dangle was fairly big and substantial (about 1½ in. across, with eight Lucite flowers backed with a metal circle), I actually joined it to the chain in four different places across the top and at both sides—rather than just one or two—for a structurally sound way of holding the earring in place. A smaller earring may not need this much support.

2. Open the jump rings and pass the first one through a section you've chosen on the back of the earring. Slip the jump ring through one link of the chain and close it securely.

3. Lay the chain flat across the back of the earring and smooth it neatly. Use a second jump ring to connect the next section of the back of the earring to the link of the chain closest to it. Close it securely.

4. Repeat this step to join the earring and chain in a few more spots, if you choose to. Trim the chain to the length you prefer and add a clasp at one end of the chain and a ring at the other.

Pair of Earrings Pendant

 **EASY**

This simplest take on the clip earring makeover uses the fun, colorful dangling sections of an old pair of earrings and reworks them—I used just half of one and all of the other, for some visual contrast and movement.

▼ **YOU'LL NEED**

Pliers

One pair of clip earrings with a two-part dangle (mine had an elongated tube above a larger round bead)

Jump rings

24-in.-long chain

Clasp and ring, plus two jump rings

FINISHED SIZE

17 in.

1. Take the earring dangles off their clips and set the clips aside. If your earrings are constructed like mine, try leaving one dangle intact and taking the top half off the other one by opening a plain loop or jump ring that connects them. (You can always rebuild them if you don't like this layout.) Hold two earrings together. I liked how mine looked paired this way, so that one large round bead was suspended well above the other, for a more unexpected arrangement. You can also leave both intact and rewire them to hang one above the other in a chain, or whatever looks best to your eye.

2. When you're happy with the arrangement, use a plain loop from the original design or a jump ring to connect the two earring dangles. Slip this loop or ring onto a chain.

3. Add a clasp at one end of the chain and a ring at the other.

Vintage Glamour Pendant

🌷 🌷 🌷 EASY

If you've seen my first jewelry-making book, Bead Simple, *you may remember one of my favorite projects, the Vintage Glamour Necklace. That elaborate piece used a beautiful sea-green and blue vintage brooch plus a single matching clip earring as the stars of a new, intricately beaded necklace design. I still have the other clip earring and wanted to make a much simpler—but no less glamorous—pendant necklace with it. Here is the sequel to that design, eight years later!*

▼ YOU'LL NEED

Pliers

One clip earring with a setting, spaces, or holes on the back that you can wire-wrap into

20-gauge wire

15 in. of chain

Clasp and ring plus two jump rings

Felt or another fabric to finish the back (optional)

Glue (optional)

Sandpaper (optional)

FINISHED SIZE

17 in.

1. Cut two 4-in. pieces of wire. Turn the earring over so the wrong side is facing up. Remove the clip using pliers if it's bulky or scratchy, and use sandpaper to sand or smooth it down if it leaves a remnant of metal.

2. Find two spaces or holes in the design you can wire into, preferably on the left and right sides or closer to the top, so it will hang nicely. Starting on the left side, use a 4-in. piece of wire to form the first half of a wrapped loop closely around one element, leaving the loop open. Repeat on the right side, making the first half of a wrapped loop there.

3. Gently tug the wire tail on each side to tighten the wrapped loops so they hug the earring's structure closely.

4. Cut the chain into two 7½-in. lengths. Form the second half of a wrapped loop on the left side of the design, slipping the last link of one piece of chain onto the open loop before you complete the wrap.

5. Repeat step 4 on the right side to add the chain and complete the wrapped loop there. Add a clasp at one end of the chain and a ring at the other. If the earring pendant is rough or uneven at the back, cut a piece of felt or another soft fabric to size and glue it down to make a smooth backing for the pendant.

Nature-Inspired Brooches & Barrettes

▶ **TECHNIQUES:**

Gluing All / **Stitching** Ribbon Rosette Clip, Briolette Flower Clips

For these three designs, I decided to reinterpret flowers in different ways, from a detailed, realistic silk-flower-turned-clip to a fancy little flower rosette in lace or even plaid wool petals. The common thread here is a super-handy backing piece that does double duty as both a hair clip and a brooch pin—perfect for making designs like this twice as wearable. I found mine, which has a smoothly curved surface to glue flowers into, at Collage in Portland, Oregon (see Resources on p. 184).

Silk Flower Simplicity Clip

● ○ ○ **EASY**

This ultra-streamlined single-blossom clip is one of my favorites—so striking in its simplicity. Choose a medium or large stand-alone silk flower to really add pop to the design, and layer a few leaves behind it if you like.

▼ **YOU'LL NEED**

Pliers
Silk flower
Sharp scissors
Hot glue and glue gun
Brooch pin/hair clip blank

FINISHED SIZE

4 in.

1. Using sharp craft scissors, cut a single silk flower blossom from the longer spray at the base of the flower so it's flush and flat. Choose a leaf or leaves from another part of the stem. Arrange the two together until you like the look, then take a photo if you like so you'll remember.

2. Using hot glue, add the leaf or leaves to the brooch pin/hair clip blank, then generously glue the flower over the leaves, pressing it into place.

3. Let cool completely before wearing in your hair or as a brooch.

Tip: *Find silk flowers by the stem at craft or floral supply stores; you can also make a hair comb with the rest of your piece (see p. 126). I used a spray of orange ranunculus, and my individual blossom measured 2½ in. across.*

Ribbon Rosette Clip

● ○ ○ **EASY**

This simple little design uses pretty materials—scalloped lace in two colors, or even plaid Pendleton wool—to make a lovely flower design crowned with a button center. Layer trims or ribbons together in a contrast pairing, or make a single fabric shine, as casual or as fancy as you like.

▼ YOU'LL NEED

Needle and thread

Lace, ribbon, or strip of torn wool fabric (see tip below)

Scissors

Hot glue and glue gun

Brooch pin/hair clip blank

Covered, sew-through, or vintage button

FINISHED SIZE

3 in.

1. Choose the materials for the flower rosette. For my lace version, I used two pieces, each measuring about 11 in. long and 1½ in. and 2 in. wide, respectively. For my wool version, I used a single strip about 16 in. long and 1 in. wide.

2. Thread a needle and knot the thread at the end. Using a running stitch, begin sewing with large stitches along one long edge of the lace or fabric. Remember, this edge will be the flower center, and the other long end will be the outer edges of the rosette.

3. Stitch until you reach the other end of the fabric strip or lace. Gently but firmly pull the thread taut, gathering the fabric closely so it forms a dramatic rosette shape. For a single-layer flower like my wool plaid, which uses a longer strip or ribbon, you can form a spiral so it overlaps itself for more stability. For a double-ribbon or lace flower, you may want to arrange it in a flatter, simpler single layer so the next piece will sit nicely.

4. When you like the arrangement of the rosette, stitch the center with a needle and thread to hold it in place and add stability. Stitch it several times and tie a knot at the end.

5. If you are making a second layer, as in my scalloped lace version, repeat this process to make the next rosette. Layer the rosettes together and hand-stitch them at the centers to join them.

6. Choose a button to add to the rosette's center, to cover the stitching as well as to complement the design. If you're using a sew-through button, stitch it on by hand. If you're using a covered or shank-style button, you can either stitch it on now or hot-glue it in the next step.

7. When you're happy with the flower, hot-glue it in place on the brooch/clip backing. If you didn't stitch the button down in step 6, hot-glue it in place.

Tip: Be sure to use a fabric or ribbon sturdy enough to hold its shape. I used two layers of the more delicate lace to give the flower more structure, but the shirt-weight wool worked beautifully on its own. I recommend using ribbon, lace, trim, or a strip of fabric at least 1 in. wide and up to about 2½ in. or 3 in. wide. Experiment and see what you like best!

Briolette Flower Clips

● ● ○ **INTERMEDIATE**

These pretty flowers are built as a circle of carefully stitched briolettes with a vintage button or rhinestone center anchoring them in place—simple, but charming! Use Lucite or acrylic briolettes rather than heavier glass, if you can find them.

▼ YOU'LL NEED

Scissors

Scrap of wool or craft felt (it will be hidden, so no need to match colors exactly)

Scrap of thick double-sided fusible interfacing such as Phoomph™

Iron (if interfacing requires it)

Hair clip (preferably with holes for stitching, but plain will work, too)

Five flat briolette-style teardrop-shaped beads drilled back to front and measuring about ¼ in. long and ½ in. wide at the widest point

Shank-style vintage button or flat-backed rhinestone

Invisible thread and hand-sewing needle

Glue

FINISHED SIZE

3 in.

1. Create a template for a ½-in.-diameter circle, and use this to cut out two circles in felt and one in double-sided fusible interfacing. Follow the interfacing directions to fuse the felt to each side of the interfacing, creating a thick three-layer circle with felt on each side.

2. Lay the briolettes out in a circular pattern like flower petals, so they're touching side to side but not overlapping. This is how you'll arrange them over the circular felt base.

3. Thread the needle with invisible thread and arrange the first bead on the felt circle. Bring the needle up from the back of the circle and stitch the first bead securely in place using at least three stitches. Add the second petal just to the right of the first and stitch it down the same way.

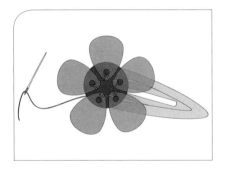

Continue stitching down the petals until you've filled the circle evenly. Tie a solid knot at the back to secure them.

4. If you're using a hair clip with holes, continue hand stitching the circle base to the clip the same way you stitched the petals down—about three stitches per spot, knotting securely at the end. If you're using a solid hair clip, push the felt base down onto a generous dab of glue and let it dry.

5. Glue a shank-style button or flat-backed rhinestone in place to cover the petals' stitching, and let it dry completely.

Tip: For briolettes like mine, I used five "petals," but you may need fewer or more depending on the width and shape you choose.

Embellished Hair Combs

▶ **TECHNIQUES:**

Wrapped Loop Winter Pearls Hair Comb, Beautiful Blossoms Hair Comb **/**
Stitching Into the Woods Fascinator **/ Gluing** Into the Woods Fascinator

These beautiful hair combs are evocative of days gone by, when a woman would arrange her hair in an elaborate style for a party, a wedding, or an evening out. Though many of us are more casual these days, making a stunning vintage-inspired hair comb to wear on a special occasion is a lot of fun. I made each of these combs using the same materials as other projects, so they match beautifully but are also economical because they use something special to its fullest—another vintage sensibility. The Winter Pearls Hair Comb, for example, features the same floral spray I used for the Winter Pearls Necklace on pp. 74–75.

Winter Pearls
Hair Comb

● ● ○ **INTERMEDIATE**

This pretty hair comb matches the Winter Pearls Necklace (see pp. 74–75)—you can make both projects from a single large floral spray from a craft store. Use any color or style of silk flowers or botanicals you like to make this project your own.

▼ **YOU'LL NEED**

Pliers

Small section of floral spray

24-gauge wire

Six beads that complement the floral spray (I used costume pearls)

Clear plastic hair comb from a beauty supply store

Glue (optional)

FINISHED SIZE

4½ in.

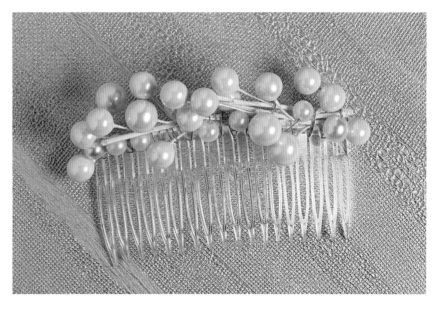

1. Cut a section of the floral spray the same length as the comb. Curve it with your fingers to follow the curve of the comb.

2. Cut a 30-in. piece of 24-gauge wire and form a wrapped loop at one end. Slip the wrapped-loop end of the wire between the first and second teeth of the comb on one end so that the loop is on the back of the comb. Run the wire tail through the loop. Don't pull it taut yet—leave a big, open loop on the front.

3. Arrange the floral spray section on the comb, tucking it into the loop so it will be caught in place when you pull it taut. Make any adjustments you like, and when you are happy with the way it looks on the front, pull the wire tightly to hold the spray in place.

4. Now loop the wire tail around the spray again, wrapping it between the second and third teeth. Continue wrapping the spray to the comb, moving from one side to the other, joining them securely. You may catch only the stem of the spray in some loops or some of the floral detail/branches in others. Just make sure it's feeling sturdy and well joined.

5. When you reach the far side of the comb, wrap the wire around the comb once and then slip a single complementary bead onto the wire tail. Begin

wrapping your way back across the comb, this time wiring beads on the front of the comb every other wrap or so to cover the earlier wire wraps and add detail to the design.

6. When you reach the end of the comb, coil the wire tail around the wrap you started with, wrapping it tightly. If necessary, add a drop of glue to secure.

Beautiful Blossoms Hair Comb

● ● ○ INTERMEDIATE

I used the same lovely burnt-orange ranunculus blossoms as the Silk Flower Simplicity Clip on p. 121 for this comb. I love the way the different sizes of blooms look together, and finishing this design with a trio of glossy faceted beads in the same beautiful color felt elegant and very, very vintage. Each of these combs will be different, depending on your materials, comb, and inspiration, so have fun making it your own!

▼ **YOU'LL NEED**

Pliers

Floral spray with generously sized blossoms on long stems

24-gauge wire

Three complementary beads (or a button or another pretty element to decorate the comb)

Vintage tortoiseshell hair comb

FINISHED SIZE

7 in.

1. Cut several of the silk flowers off the main spray, leaving stems of 3 in. to 5 in., if possible. I used four flowers of different sizes and one set of leaves for my comb.

2. Come up with a simple overall design for your comb. I oriented my two larger flowers on the right side, balancing them by placing my two smaller flowers on the left side with all the stems facing toward the center. You can cover these stems with the

flowers themselves in the final design, but make sure that you have plenty of length to work with.

3. Cut a 30-in. piece of 24-gauge wire and form a wrapped loop at one end. Slip the wrapped-loop end of the wire between the first and second teeth of the comb on one end so that the loop is on the back of the comb. Run the wire tail through the loop. Don't pull it taut yet—leave a big, open loop on the front.

4. Arrange the first larger flower stem on the comb, tucking it well into the loop so it will be caught in place when you pull it taut. Make any adjustments that you like, and when you are happy with the way it looks on the front, pull the wire tightly to hold the spray in place.

5. Loop the wire tail around the spray again, wrapping it in the same spot.

Make repeated wraps for a heavier, multiple-flower arrangement like this one—I like to wrap three times per space between teeth for this style. Continue wrapping and add the second flower blossom and stem to the comb, moving from one side to the other, joining the flowers to the comb securely. In my design, the second flower was the largest, so I made sure to wrap it tightly and completely cover the stem of the first flower with it. Make any adjustments so the two blossoms look their best together.

6. Continue wrapping toward the left side of the comb, adding the third (in my case, smaller) flower blossom and stem with its stem facing the center. Don't worry if there's an area where the stem and wire show; just make sure that the wrapping is secure and strong.

7. Slip a final flower blossom into the design at the left end of the comb, if you like, and wire it on neatly. Add a set of leaves behind the final flower and adjust it to complement the overall design.

8. Move back toward the center and begin to wire the complementary beads or button in place to cover the stem area you may have left exposed where the flowers have a natural gap or space. Be creative here. When you are happy with the appearance, carefully coil the wire tail around the wraps at the back, making sure there are no rough edges poking out.

Into the Woods Fascinator
by Kayte Terry

● ● ○ **INTERMEDIATE**

If there's one thing I've learned as a maker, it's save your scraps! These little bits and bobs may seem destined for the trash, but, with the right project, they are transformed into treasure. I imagine this fascinator, made from scraps in my studio and inspired by fall foliage, as a crown to the perfect autumnal outfit.

▼ YOU'LL NEED

Leather scraps
Small pieces of leather cord
Awl or hole-punch pliers
Scrap of wood
Wool plaid scraps
Wool felt scrap
Tailor's chalk or fabric marker
Fabric scissors

Permanent jewel or embellishment glue such as Fabri-Tac™
Hair comb
Needle and thread
Sequins or embellishments (optional)

FINISHED SIZE

4 in.

1. Roughly cut out a 4-in.-long oval from the wool felt scrap. This will be the base of the fascinator. It will be totally covered up with embellishments, so it doesn't have to be perfect!

2. Draw flower and leaf shapes onto the wrong side of leather scraps with tailor's chalk or a fabric marker. Cut out a variety of these with fabric scissors.

3. To layer the leather flowers, lay leather flower pieces one at a time on a scrap of wood and punch a hole through the centers with an awl or hole-punch pliers.

4. Thread the leather cord through the flower layers. Tie a knot on the right side of the flowers in the centers. Trim the cord on the wrong side of the flowers and secure the end of the cord to the bottom of the flower with glue.

5. Cut several 2-in. circles out of the wool plaid fabric.

6. Lay the wool circles and the leather flowers onto the felt base of the fascinator. Make sure you have the perfect arrangement, then start gluing the pieces down. You may need more or fewer felt circles depending on your layout and how densely you layer the components.

7. Thread a needle and sew the comb to the felt base of the fascinator. Add sequins or other embellishments to your fascinator, if desired.

Geometric Brooches & Barrettes

▶ **TECHNIQUES:**

Gluing All / **Cross-Stitching** Square-within-a-Square Brooch

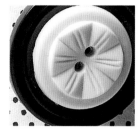

This eye-catching set of brooches and barrettes presents the most basic of geometric shapes in an impactful way. Whether you make fun custom covered buttons with your favorite fabric prints, layer vintage buttons for high-contrast loveliness, or stitch your own square-within-a-square design to draw the eye, you'll love these easy-to-make, fun-to-wear projects.

Covered-Button Barrettes

● ○ ○ **EASY**

Like the geometric Covered-Button Pendant (see p. 111), this project is a perfect way to use even the smallest fabric scraps. I made one larger clip and one smaller bobby- pin style, but you can mix and match yours any way you like.

▼ **YOU'LL NEED**

Pliers

One covered-button kit

Small pieces of fabric of your choice—I recommend a non-directional or multidirectional print, with details small enough so you can capture them within the button's face

Scissors

Glue

Plain sew-through-style button that fits behind the covered button, one for each clip you're making

Bobby pin or hair clip

FINISHED SIZE

3 in.

1. Use pliers to remove the shank from the button backing. Following the covered-button kit package directions and template, cut out a fabric circle for each button.

2. Create one covered button, following the package directions.

Apply a generous dab of glue right into the back of the covered button and press the plain sew-through button into it. Let it set until the glue is mostly or completely dry and the inner button does not easily move.

3. Once the glue is set, use another generous dab of glue to attach the covered button to the hair clip or bobby pin. Let it dry completely before wearing.

Tip: Do not use cute, inspirational buttons for the sew-through buttons— these behind-the-scenes buttons should be workhorses, not ballerinas.

Vintage Buttons Brooch

● ○ ○ **EASY**

I paired two eye-catching round vintage buttons for this striking little brooch. You could make it as a hair clip if you prefer, too. Look for Lucite, casein, or plastic buttons rather than heavier glass or solid metal, so they don't weigh down your coat (or your hairdo).

▼ **YOU'LL NEED**

Two vintage buttons, sew-through style (I used a 1³/₄-in. black button for the base and a 1¹/₈-in. white button for the focal button)

Glue

Pin back or clip base

FINISHED SIZE

2 in.

1. Find two vintage or new buttons you like together, one larger than the other, and arrange the smaller one over the larger. You should be able to see a rim of the base button around the smaller one, for visual contrast.

2. Glue the smaller button in place over the larger button and let the glue set. (You can also stitch them together if you like, but I found the glue had a stronger hold than even the most careful stitching.)

3. Flip the buttons over and glue the pin back or clip to the back, centering it neatly. Let dry completely before wearing.

Square-within-a-Square Brooch

● ● ○ **INTERMEDIATE**

When I'm not making jewelry, I love to make modern quilts, and one of my favorite block patterns is the venerable log cabin. I reinterpreted the square-within-a-square block setting here in cross-stitch and thought it was fun as a little brooch or pin for a tote bag. I'm giving general directions here, since the wooden blanks may vary in size or shape, but make this project your own with the colors, design, and finishing touches you like best.

▼ YOU'LL NEED

Square wooden blank with pre-drilled holes (I used one that was 1⅔ in. across from Fabric Depot in Portland, Oregon; see Resources on p. 184)

Pencil

Three or more colors of pearl cotton or embroidery floss

Needle

Pin back or hair clip

Felt

Scissors

FINISHED SIZE

Width: 2 in.

1. Choose at least three fun colors of pearl cotton (a neatly twisted thick single cord) or embroidery floss (usually, six strands of thin threads) that contrast well together. I chose some of my favorite colors for this little quilt block—coral, gray, and aqua.

2. Thread a needle with the first color of floss or cotton to stitch the perimeter of the design. I used a single strand of pearl cotton or two strands of embroidery floss for my stitching.

3. Fill in the outer rim of the stitching area with cross-stitch ✕s, moving clockwise around the wooden blank. There are many good cross-stitch tutorials and books that can offer detailed instructions, but see the instructions on p. 32 to get started.

4. Continue stitching ✕s around the perimeter of the wooden blank, catching the thread tail inside the back of your stitching for security. Stitch two full rows around the perimeter in background thread. When you've finished, guide the needle through a row of stitching on the back of the blank

and pull it through so that the thread is caught in place like a knot.

5. Thread the needle with the second color and stitch two more rows inside the first two, working from the outside in. This will go faster, since the rows are shorter!

Stitch to fill the center square with the third color (or repeat the outer square color if you'd like to).

6. Glue felt over the stitching at the back of the wooden blank. Glue a pin back or hair clip securely to the felt, centering it.

Tip: See the Cross-Stitch Pendant on p. 114 for an initials design that's another take on this same idea.

Semiprecious Brooches & Barrettes

▶ **TECHNIQUES:**

Gluing Coral Cross Brooch / **Wrapped Loop** Semiprecious Barrettes, Stylish Sweater Clips

Using semiprecious stones or cabochons for these special projects lends a luxurious vintage sensibility to basic little wearables. Use your favorite stones for these barrettes, sweater clips, and brooches, or make a very personal gift for a friend to enjoy.

Coral Cross Brooch

● ○ ○ **EASY**

This simple brooch is made similarly to the geometric Vintage Buttons Brooch (see p. 129), with a large, flat button as the base. You can often find inexpensive large buttons made for coats at thrift stores or rummage sales—don't glue onto a valuable or favorite button, but instead use a simple, plain one that could use a little pick-me-up.

▼ **YOU'LL NEED**

Glue

Large flat-back round button

Four oval cabochons (I used imitation coral scarabs)

Pin back or hair clip

FINISHED SIZE

2 in.

1. Decide which side of the button you want to use as the base of the brooch. I actually used the back of mine, which was perfectly smooth, instead of the front, which had a decorative rim. Place the four cabochons on it in a cross formation. Mine lined up neatly size-wise, but if yours extend off, that could be an interesting design element! (See the Framed Floral Pendant on p. 108 for an example of marquise/oval shapes that go beyond the boundaries of a jewelry piece.)

2. Once you're happy with the cabochons' placement, carefully lift them up one at a time and glue them down securely. Let them dry completely before moving the brooch.

3. Glue a pin back or hair clip to the back and let it dry completely.

Design Principles: Mixing High and Low Materials

This is a very flexible idea—for example, if you use inexpensive bright-colored buttons as one of the major materials in a necklace, elevate them with good-quality sterling silver wire, chain, and findings. Or put a few intricate vintage charms on a simple, narrow ribbon. Mixing the formal and the casual however works best can be an intriguing way to make your pieces unique. The inexpensive barrette clips in this project, for example, are elevated beyond imagination by the semiprecious gems.

Semiprecious Barrettes

● ● ○ **INTERMEDIATE**

This barrette showcases gorgeous semiprecious stones in a neat, organized row. Keeping them simple, with no other ornamentation or extras, really lets them shine. You can either use all one style of beads, like my carnelians, or mix two complementary shapes, as I did in the variation, like smaller rounds and ovals in gray agate and smoky quartz. I personally like ovals as a design element, but use whatever shape you are drawn to.

▼ **YOU'LL NEED**

Pliers

24-gauge craft wire

Semiprecious beads of your choice (I used four ³/₄-in.-long oval carnelians for one barrette and four ¹/₂-in. smoky quartz ovals with six ¹/₄-in. gray agate rounds for my other one)

Flat-topped spring barrette with small holes at each end—mine was about 3 in. wide

FINISHED SIZE

3 in.

1. Lay out semiprecious beads you like in a row. You may want to angle wider beads, like my oval carnelians, so they fit on the barrette neatly. This is a flexible design.

2. Cut a 16-in. piece of craft wire and make a wrapped loop at one end. Working from the back, pass the wire tail through one of the holes at one end of the barrette, and then slip it through

the loop, pulling it taut. Pull the wire tail to the front of the barrette so the wrapped loop and overlap are at the back and firmly held in place.

3. Working from that end of the barrette toward the center, put the first semiprecious bead on the wire and angle it into place so it's flush with the end of the wire. Wrap the wire tail around the barrette top twice, pulling it taut and even, so the bead is neatly caught between the original starting place and the two wire wraps.

4. To make a patterned barrette like the agate and quartz design, start with one bead like my quartz oval, wiring it on the same way, then introduce the alternate one after the two wraps. I strung two smaller agates on as one unit, then wrapped twice, added a

second quartz oval, and so on until I reached the far side of the barrette.

5. Repeat step 3 to add more beads, wrapping twice between each of them, until you reach the other end of the barrette.

6. Slip the wire tail through the small hole at this end and wrap it securely three or four times. Tuck the wire securely under the beads, pull it taut, and trim it so no sharp ends protrude.

Tip: Try not to use stones and beads that are too heavy, or the barrette won't be comfortable to wear.

Stylish Sweater Clips

● ● ○ **INTERMEDIATE**

I love to wear cardigan sweaters, and these little beaded clips are such a nice extra to dress them up a bit. You can use any semiprecious beads you like here. I used costume pearls for one and some of the same carnelians from Semiprecious Barrettes (see p. 133) for the other. I like my sweater clips to measure 4 in. to 7 in. across, but it's up to you, and your beads, how you want to design yours.

▼ **YOU'LL NEED**

Pliers

24-gauge wire

Semiprecious beads of your choice (I used four ¾-in. carnelian ovals for one clip that measured 6 in. across and five 7-mm costume pearls for a shorter clip that measured 4½ in. across)

Two clips

FINISHED SIZE

4½ in. to 6 in. (adjustable)

1. Cut 4-in. pieces of wire, one for each bead you plan to use in your sweater clip chain. Form the first half of a wrapped loop at one end of the first piece of wire and slip it onto the first clip. Complete the wrap to join it securely.

2. Slip a bead onto the wire and make a wrapped loop on the other side to make it a bead connector, joined to the clip.

3. Continue making the beads into wrapped-loop bead connectors, working from left to right, joining each one to the bead chain before completing the wrap. Finish by connecting the right-side bead to the second clip and completing the wrap securely.

My Favorite Brooches & Barrettes

▶ **TECHNIQUES:**

Gluing Butterfly Brooch, Bow Tie Brooch / **Stitching** Bow Tie Brooch / **Wrapped Loop** Safety Pin Tassel Charm Brooch

All three of these brooch designs deliver gorgeous style, from a vintage-inspired butterfly to a gleaming gold tassel and charm, plus a charming little bow tie and floral cabochon pairing that draws the eye instantly. Use these as inspiration to make your own instant favorites!

Butterfly Brooch

● ○ ○ **EASY**

This darling little yellow butterfly I found at a thrift store reminds me of my 1970s childhood, and I knew it had to become something special. It flutters over a simple burnt-orange Bakelite button, but you can use any style of butterfly, and any setting that suits it best. Wear this brooch when you need an extra dose of charm.

▼ **YOU'LL NEED**

Butterfly charm
Flat-backed button (I used a Bakelite button that measured 1³/₄ in.) or another setting
Glue
Pin back or clip base

FINISHED SIZE

2 in.

1. Glue the butterfly charm onto the button or other setting. Let it dry completely.

2. Glue the pin back or clip base onto the center of the back of the button.

Safety Pin Tassel Charm Brooch by Christina Batch-Lee

● ● ○ **INTERMEDIATE**

I love the versatility of this project: It can be used as a brooch or scarf pin, add a little drama to a plain purse, or even serve as a special topper to a gift. It's a great way to showcase charms that are meaningful to you or to your gift recipient.

▼ **YOU'LL NEED**

Extra-large safety pin or kilt pin (mine measures 2 in. long)
Desired charms
Large jump ring for each charm (I used 10 mm)
30 in. of chain
One 6-mm jump ring
12-mm bead cap to fit over chain
20-gauge brass wire (or eyepin) about 2¹/₂ in. long
Pliers

FINISHED SIZE

5¹/₂ in.

1. Create the tassel charm by cutting the chain into 12 equal lengths, measuring approximately 2¹/₂ in. each. Open the 6-mm jump ring and slip one end of each chain length onto the ring. Close the jump ring securely.

2. Using round-nose pliers, round one end of the brass wire and attach it to the jump ring holding the chains. Slip the bead cap onto the straight end of the wire. To close, create a wrapped loop at the top of the bead cap. Coil the wire end around the base of the wire to finish. Snip excess wire close to the base.

3. Attach each charm to the base of the safety pin with a large jump ring.

Tip: For a simple variation, you can also use a premade fabric or leather tassel from a fashion trim store in place of the chain.

Bow Tie Brooch by Michelle Freedman

● ● ○ **INTERMEDIATE**

Add a little *ooh-la-la* to any outfit with this romantic bow tie brooch. Vintage cabochons are the perfect ingredient for repurposed accent pieces. The secret to this design is attaching a pendant bail to hold the hand-stitched fabric bow. Match your cabochon with a classic black-and-white stripe, whimsical polka dot, or your favorite sparkly fabric to personalize your look.

▼ YOU'LL NEED

Cabochon of your choice, 1 in. or larger

Pendant bail with an offset loop

Glue that works with multiple surfaces, including metal

Bar pin brooch blank with 25-mm round clear pad

Fabric

Hand-sewing needle

Straight pin

All-purpose thread

FINISHED SIZE

1½ in. and 2½ in.

1. Affix the bar pin brooch blank to the back of the cabochon with glue. Make sure there is room for the pendant bail at the top before you set it to dry.

2. When the bar pin is dry, make a small mark on the back of the piece where the center of the pendant bail will go. The loop should be at the top of the cabochon. Affix the pendant bail to the back of the cabochon with the glue and let it dry.

3. For a large bow, cut a piece of fabric 4 in. wide by 6 in. long. Fold each 6-in. raw edge to the center, overlapping ¼ in. where they meet. Thread one short end of the folded fabric through the pendant bail loop and pull it halfway through.

4. For a smaller bow, cut a piece of fabric 2¼ in. wide by 4½ in. long. Fold the short ends into the center of the fabric so they overlap ¼ in. (Note: You may need to pull the fabric through the pendant bail loop first before folding it.) Place a straight pin across the center to hold the layers together.

5. Thread a needle and tie a strong knot at one end of the thread. Sew several rows of running stitches where the short ends overlap in the center of the bow. Pull tightly so it gathers in the center. Make sure to stitch through all layers so the back pieces are stitched through to the front pieces. Secure with a short backstitch or strong knot when you finish.

6. Use your fingers to fluff the bow and even out the ends. Pin to your favorite sweater or button-down shirt.

Vintage Gone Modern Brooches & Barrettes

▶ TECHNIQUES: **Gluing** All

These colorful little hair clips and hairpins put a simple, modern spin on a vintage standby. Pair sparkles, beads, or buttons with filigree or molded flowers in your favorite colors and glue them on to sturdy metal clips or slides for a perfect marriage of old and new. ❦

Filigree Flowers Hairpin

 **EASY**

These delicate, pretty filigree pieces look so good with embellished centers. I used flat-backed rhinestones in spring colors to finish my metal flowers, but a button or any other embellishment you prefer would be lovely, too.

▼ YOU'LL NEED

One flat-backed rhinestone or button

One filigree flower

One bobby pin

Cement glue

Strong glue

FINISHED SIZE

3 in.

1. Apply a generous dab of cement glue to the back of the rhinestone and glue it to the center of a filigree flower. Let it set, and then glue the layered flower design to a bobby pin with strong glue. Let dry completely before wearing.

Floral Hair Clips

 **EASY**

This version uses a larger scale and bigger hair clips, but the assembly is just as easy. Add bead or button centers to premade ribbon flowers, more dramatic filigree pieces, or anything else that catches your eye.

▼ YOU'LL NEED

One button or bead

One large filigree flower or ribbon flower piece

One large hair clip

Strong glue

FINISHED SIZE

4 in.

1. Choose a center element and glue it to the middle of a ribbon or metal filigree flower component. Let it set, then apply a generous dab of glue to the back of each flower and attach it to a large hair clip. Let dry completely before wearing.

Solo Floral Hairpins

 **EASY**

This simplest version just calls for flower cabochons, or any pieces with flat backs, to stand alone in an instant-favorite design.

▼ YOU'LL NEED

One flat-backed flower or other cabochon pieces

One bobby pin

Strong glue

FINISHED SIZE

3 in.

1. Make sure the back of the cabochon is clean, dry, and flat. Apply a generous dab of glue to the back and glue it to a bobby pin. Let dry completely before wearing. That's it!

Charm Bracelet Deluxe

▶ **TECHNIQUES:**

Jump Rings All / **Plain Loops** Beads & Briolettes Charm Bracelet /
Wrapped Loops Beads & Briolettes Charm Bracelet

When I was a little girl, I loved playing with my mom's charm bracelet from her jewelry box. She lived in Europe for a year as a teenager and found all kinds of beautiful souvenirs of the places she and her family visited. One of my favorites was a tiny beer stein whose lid opened and closed! Now I love making my own charm bracelets, from the traditional version crowded with jingling little treasures to a fancy collection of beads on a dramatic oversize chain. No matter what style you're most drawn to, make this bracelet your own!

Minimal Initials Charm Bracelet

● ○ ○ **EASY**

You may have seen pendants like this—a collection of charms with initials or names representing your children or all your family members—but I liked the idea of making a charm bracelet instead. I found a cool little set of lightweight initial charms that look like vintage type-writer keys and added one for Pearl and Everett. Now they think their bracelet is the best project in the book!

▼ **YOU'LL NEED**

Pliers

Oversize chain (I used a copper circle chain)

Initial charms or other meaningful pieces

Jump rings for each charm

Magnetic clasp plus two jump rings

FINISHED SIZE

7 in.

1. Choose two (or a few) initial charms you love and arrange them together. Make sure they're not too heavy; for a simple design like this, bigger or heavier pieces will pull the bracelet sharply down.

2. Cut the chain to the desired length for your wrist (mine was 6½ in. long), and lay it out flat. Open the jump rings and set all but one aside.

3. Place the initials in the spots you choose. I put mine together on links that were side by side closer to one end of the bracelet. You can center yours, space them out farther, or position them however you like. Attach the first charm to the bracelet with the jump ring and close it securely.

4. Repeat to join any other charms to the bracelet. Add the magnetic clasp to the ends of the bracelet with jump rings.

Design Principles: Mixing Metals

Sometimes mixing metals is intentional, and to be perfectly honest, sometimes it means the difference between wearing something today and waiting until I can make a special trip to the bead store for the "right" finding. Either way, mixing copper, brass, silver, or gold together lends a lighthearted and interesting element to your work, as well as a nice dose of visual texture that makes a certain statement. Conversely, use matching metals for a rich and harmonious effect. It's up to you!

Beads & Briolettes Charm Bracelet

 ● ○ ○ **EASY**

Like the Minimal Initials Charm Bracelet (see the facing page), this design also uses oversize circle chain to spotlight an assortment of pretty little handmade bead charms in a beautiful setting. I used clear beads and attached one charm to each link of the chain, but you can mix and match colors or add more charms if you like for a lush effect.

▼ YOU'LL NEED

Pliers

Oversize chain that lies flat (I used a gold circle chain)

10 clear faceted round pearl beads

Four clear briolettes

24-gauge wire

Seed beads

Magnetic clasp plus two jump rings

FINISHED SIZE

7 in.

1. Plan your bracelet design. I made a simple repeating pattern for my bracelet, but you can randomize your design if you prefer.

2. Cut one 3-in. piece of wire (or the length needed) for each bead or briolette. Form briolette wraps (see p. 25) above any teardrop-shaped bead and form the first half of a wrapped loop above each one. Place a seed bead above the first half of the coil.

3. Form a plain loop on each piece of wire that will become a bead dangle/charm. Slip a bead onto a piece of wire, then slip on a seed bead. Form the first half of a wrapped loop above the beads and set it aside. Repeat with all remaining beads.

4. Cut the chain to 6½ in. or the length desired and lay out the charms. Add the first charm to the first circle of chain, facing front, and complete the wrap.

5. Continue adding beads and briolettes in the order you prefer until you reach the opposite side of the bracelet. Add a magnetic clasp with jump rings.

Modern Traditional Charm Bracelet

● ○ ○   **EASY**

I made this charm bracelet when I was in my 20s, drawing on everything from my favorite little stars to a tiny, perfect sterling silver sewing machine to celebrate that I'd just fallen in love with sewing. Instead of strictly limiting myself to charms, I mixed in lockets, lucky bits and pieces, and even my high school graduation year charm, right off the tassel. Choose a sturdy chain with links that lie flat, and arrange the charms evenly by size and weight for a successful finished design.

▼ YOU'LL NEED

Pliers

Sturdy chain with links big enough to pass a jump ring through, preferably with links that lie flat

Charms of your choice (I used a total of 15)

One jump ring for each charm

Clasp plus two jump rings

Digital camera (optional)

FINISHED SIZE

7 in.

1. Open a jump ring for each charm and set them aside. Cut the chain to 6½ in. or the desired length for your wrist.

2. Arrange the charms in an order you like. Be sure to mix heavier and lighter weights together so no one section of the bracelet is under too much pressure from heavy elements. When you've finished arranging, take a digital photo so you'll remember the design, in case it gets ruffled.

3. Attach one jump ring to each charm, then begin attaching charms to the links of the bracelet, spacing them fairly evenly. Close each jump ring securely. Add a clasp to one end of the charm bracelet and a ring to the other.

Tip: Be creative when choosing your favorite charms and lucky bits and pieces to wear together, whether they're smashed pennies you collect, souvenirs of favorite places, or meaningful symbols or good luck charms. I mixed vintage and new pieces and all different metals throughout. Just make sure everything can be attached via a jump ring (for example, drill a small hole into a smashed penny or another flat object) and isn't so fragile it could be ruined by everyday wear alongside other charms (like a delicate glass piece).

Nature-Inspired Bracelets

▶ **TECHNIQUES:**

Jump Rings Leaves on Chain Bracelet, Feathers Bracelet / **Gluing** Button Blossoms Bracelet

These link bracelets bring a bit of the natural world into their simple but effective repeating designs. I looked for pretty metal filigree and charm pieces and took my cues from them, mixing metals and textures for a stylish but slightly unexpected result, just like nature itself.

Leaves on Chain Bracelet

● ○ ○ EASY

Another take on a charm bracelet, this piece came to life when I found brass leaves clustered together on an old broken necklace. I knew they'd be chic when given a little room to breathe. The decorative chain I found for my bracelet's base offered a perfect setting for adding little groups of leaves separated by a longer link, as leaves often grow on branches of a tree. Mixing brass and copper gave it a warm and inviting feel.

▼ YOU'LL NEED

Pliers

7 in. of decorative chain (or desired length)

15 leaf charms, drilled back to front

Fifteen 4-mm jump rings (one per charm)

Magnetic clasp plus two jump rings

FINISHED SIZE

7 in.

1. Create your leaf groupings. Open the jump rings and begin adding the charms to the chain one by one, working from side to side. I made my pattern completely symmetrical, but you can randomize or alternate your groupings. I added three leaves per decorative link, leaving spaces for contrast.

2. Once you've finished adding charms and like the effect, use the last two jump rings to add the magnetic clasp halves at both ends.

Feathers Bracelet

● ○ ○ EASY

This chain was inspired by feather charms I found that were drilled at both ends so they could act as working connectors rather than just ornaments. I built the chain with sturdy jump rings, then added a pair of feathers with contrast metals as a small embellishment.

▼ YOU'LL NEED

Pliers

Nine silver ⅔-in.-long feather or other nature-themed charms drilled at both ends

Eight 6-mm or 8-mm jump rings to connect them, depending on size of charms

Two small contrast feather charms, one brass and one copper

Two 4-mm jump rings (one per charm)

Magnetic clasp plus two 4-mm jump rings

FINISHED SIZE

7 in.

1. Lay out the double-drilled charms end to end. Open each 6-mm jump ring and slip the bottom of one feather charm and the top of another feather charm onto the first open ring. Close it securely.

2. Continue linking the feather charms with large jump rings, always joining the bottom of one to the top of the

next for symmetry. Leave the first and last feather charms' outer ends open for now.

3. Choose a spot to add the embellishment feather charms and attach them there using 4-mm jump rings. I added mine off center, between my sixth and seventh feather charm links, on a large jump ring.

4. Attach the magnetic clasp halves to each end of the bracelet using 4-mm jump rings.

Tip: Find leaf charms you like, whether they're identical like mine or assorted sizes, metals, or styles. I used a total of 15, in five small groups, all the way around my bracelet, but you can arrange yours any way you'd like.

Tip: Choose a chain that works nicely with the charms. You can either use a decorative chain like mine, which pairs S-curve links with longer solid links, or use a more traditional chain and leave spaces at intervals.

Button Blossoms Bracelet

 ○ ○ **EASY**

A flat-link metal bracelet blank is perfect for embellishing, and these three-dimensional filigree flowers work perfectly on a sturdy, almost completely hidden base. A pretty good color match of bright golds keeps your attention on the more elaborate flowers and joyful yellow button centers, giving the bracelet lots of life while keeping things very organized, too.

▼ YOU'LL NEED

Bracelet blank with six links (or length desired)

Six 1-in. filigree flowers

Six small sew-through buttons or other embellishments like sequins or rhinestones

Glue

FINISHED SIZE

7 in.

1. Apply generous dabs of glue to each of the bracelet links and press the filigree flowers into them one by one. Let them set, checking to make sure the flowers don't slide off their centers as the glue dries.

2. Add small dabs of glue at the center of each flower and press a button into each one. Let the bracelet dry completely before wearing it.

Tip: Lay the bracelet blank out flat and audition filigree pieces for size and placement. If you find one component first and want to build a design around that element, take it to a bead shop or measure it for ordering online.

Semiprecious Bracelets

▶ **TECHNIQUES:**

Bead Stringing Semiprecious Charm Bracelets, Carnelian & Gold Bracelet /
Crimp Beads Semiprecious Charm Bracelets, Carnelian & Gold Bracelet /
Plain Loops Cabochons & Rounds Bracelet

I turned to some favorite stones for these bracelets, like endlessly lovely carnelian with all of its markings and color gradations, a striking little pairing of pearl and lapis as the focal points in an overall design, and vintage faux coral as vivid as the real thing. Whether you make something simple and beautiful so the semi-precious beads shine or make something more intricate, have fun using these timelessly beautiful materials for something special.

Tip: Never be afraid to substitute faux stones for real semiprecious materials. Whether it's for ethical reasons—for example, much of the world's coral is now endangered, so imitation coral is certainly a solid choice—or just because you like vintage costume pearls, substitutions can be as beautiful and meaningful as the original ones. Good-quality beads and stones are important, of course, but being flexible in what you use is important, too!

Semiprecious Charm Bracelets

● ○ ○ **EASY**

The semiprecious "charms" here are strung right into a simple background of red jasper beads—a beautiful but understated setting. I like the way the two bracelets work together, with the pearl and lapis moving freely around the perimeters. A magnetic clasp on each will hold your bead charms in place neatly.

▼ **YOU'LL NEED**

Tape

Soft Flex wire

A strand of small semiprecious beads (I used red jasper in natural shapes)

One or more charms to mix into your designs

Two crimp beads per strand

Magnetic clasp

Flat-nose pliers

FINISHED SIZE

7 in.

1. Plan a design 6½ in. long (or desired length), thinking about where you'd like to place your charms. I put my charms near one end, about 2 in. in, with some variation. Remember, if you use magnetic clasps, they'll attract one another, so space the charms accordingly.

2. Cut a 12-in. piece of Soft Flex wire and double a piece of tape at one end. Begin threading small semiprecious beads onto the wire one by one, and when you reach the spot you've chosen for your charm, string that on as if it's a bead, or place it on with its jump ring if it's a dangle. Continue beading as you move toward the other end of the bracelet and stop when you've reached your desired length.

3. Add one crimp bead on the Soft Flex wire and add one half of a magnetic clasp there. Guide the wire back through the crimp bead and the first few beads, leaving a tail. Crimp the bead flat with flat-nose pliers.

4. Take the tape off the other end of the Soft Flex wire and repeat step 3 to add the other half of the clasp there with a crimp bead, too.

Carnelian & Gold Bracelet

● ○ ○ **EASY**

This simple setting allows the red agates to showcase their beautiful color gradations and markings to the fullest. Gold seed beads add warmth and shine to their gorgeous tone.

▼ **YOU'LL NEED**

Pliers

18 carnelian beads (I used rondelles with faceted sides)

19 large gold glass seed beads

Soft Flex wire

Tape

Two crimp beads

Magnetic clasp

FINISHED SIZE

7 in.

1. Cut a 12-in. length of Soft Flex wire and add tape to one end. Choose a simple repeating pattern—mine just alternates between a carnelian bead and a seed bead—and begin stringing the semiprecious beads in that design. The nice thing about Soft Flex wire is that you can easily try out patterns and then take beads off to finalize your design.

2. Once you've strung enough beads to finish your bracelet to 6½ in. (or the length you prefer), add a crimp bead and then half of a magnetic clasp. Thread the wire back through the crimp bead and the last few beads, flatten the crimp bead, and trim the wire tail.

3. Take the tape off the first side and repeat to add the other half of the clasp.

Cabochons & Rounds Bracelet

● ○ ○   **EASY**

I found these vintage faux-coral cabochons with detailed scarab markings at a bead store and knew I wanted to mix the bright orange-red ovals with something completely different for contrast. I found smooth, cool aventurine rounds and thought they'd look beautiful together. My cabochons were neatly encased in metal settings, making it easy to join them with plain loops, but you can re-create this look with oval beads or another elongated style that gives the same interesting effect.

▼ YOU'LL NEED

Pliers

Four cabochons in settings with loops on either end for wire-work, or other elongated beads (I used vintage scarabs in faux coral)

Five round beads in a different color or stone for a striking contrast (I used aventurine rounds)

20-gauge wire

Magnetic clasp

FINISHED SIZE

6½ in.

1. Cut the 20-gauge wire into five 2-in. pieces and turn each of the smaller round beads into a bead connector with plain loops on each side. If the cabochons need loops to connect them, cut the wire and turn those into connectors the same way.

2. Alternating round beads and cabochons, join the beads together by carefully opening plain loops, then closing them securely once they're linked. Begin and end with a plain-loop bead. Add a magnetic clasp half to each end of the bracelet design.

Tip: Choose two very different semi-precious beads or jewelry components for an interesting contrast. I loved the hot orange-red of the faux coral and the cool green of the aventurine together. I tried a few different combinations and settled on simply alternating them one by one around a bracelet.

Design Principles: Color, Color, Color!

Color is powerful, whether it suggests warmth, coolness, a look back at the past, an of-the-moment, on-trend inspiration, or any other message you're drawn to. Keep your projects monochromatic for a consistent, strong feel, or mix two complementary hues for a piece that's easy on the eyes. Reach across the color wheel (see p. 15) for something that packs more of a punch, or draw your inspiration from the outside world or the entire spectrum—it's up to you!

Geometric Bracelets

▶ **TECHNIQUES:**

Knotting Wood Squares Bracelet / **Gluing** Wood Squares Bracelet, Circle Cabochons Bracelet / **Bead Stringing** Angular Hexagons Bracelet / **Crimp Beads** Angular Hexagons Bracelet

Each of these flexible link bracelets employs a different geometric shape to encircle your wrist with a strong repeating design. Whether you're drawn to the organic calm of wood squares, the simplicity of round vintage cabochons, or the unexpected movement of angular, elongated hexagons with tiny cube beads sliding inside, you'll love wearing these striking pieces.

Wood Squares Bracelet

● ● ○ **INTERMEDIATE**

As with the Gold & Coral Necklace (see p. 87), these smooth, substantial beads are brought to life with an unexpected pop of color in the knotted silk thread that unites them. I used the same coral thread left over from my gold necklace, but go in any color direction you like for this simple, impactful design.

▼ YOU'LL NEED

Tweezers

Glue

Pliers

One card of silk beading cord (I used size 12) in bright coral, or leftovers from another project

Two bead tips

Seven ³/₄-in.-long square flat wooden beads

Beading board (optional)

Magnetic clasp (plus jump rings if needed)

FINISHED SIZE

6¹/₂ in.

1. Lay the square beads out in a row from left to right. If you have small size discrepancies, as I did, mix the beads so they form a pattern or look appealing.

2. Unwind the silk beading cord from its card and stretch it out. Tie a single knot 2 in. from the end. Add a bead tip to the strand so that the cupping halves face away from the needle and toward the knot, then use tweezers to position a single knot just above the bead tip, pulling it taut.

3. Slip the first square bead onto the cord and position it just above the knot. Add another knot above the first bead. Add more beads in the order you set them out. When you add the last bead, make one more knot just above it to hold it in place.

4. Add the second bead tip onto the cord, so the cups are facing away from the beads. Tie a single knot inside the cups, again using the tweezers to position it neatly.

5. Cut the excess cord from the ends of the bracelet, close to the bead-tip knots. Add a drop of glue to each knot to seal it, and then use flat-nose pliers to close the bead tips over the knots.

6. Add the clasp to one bead tip and curve it closed using round-nose pliers. Add the second half to the other side the same way.

Tip: Beading cord is sold in different thicknesses, much like wire. The smaller the number, the thinner the cord is. My beads were drilled generously, so I used a 12. Make sure the cord can easily pass through each bead, but a single knot should stop it in its tracks so it can't slip over to bump its neighbor.

Circle Cabochons Bracelet

 ○ ○ **EASY**

I found these vintage Japanese plastic floral cabochons in a lot of old jewelry bits and separated out two sizes—some were ⅔ in. across and others were about ½ in. I found enough to alternate between smaller and larger on an 11-link bracelet blank, creating a simple, colorful, lightweight bracelet that offers lots of pop. Use bright buttons or any other flat-backed cabochons for a similar look and feel.

▼ YOU'LL NEED

Bracelet blank (mine was smaller in scale and had 11 links)

11 flat-backed cabochons of your choice (1 per bracelet link)

Strong glue

FINISHED SIZE

7 in.

1. Lay out the cabochons in the order that appeals to you. I alternated between smaller and larger sizes, beginning and ending with a smaller cabochon.

2. Working from left to right, glue the cabochons down securely, one to each link, and let them dry completely, checking your project midway through to make sure the cabochons haven't slipped off center.

Angular Hexagons Bracelet

● ○ ○ **EASY**

I found these simple double-drilled metal hexagons and immediately pictured them with tiny beads moving inside the negative space like an abacus. Tiny glass cubes in a high-contrast acid green worked beautifully with the antiqued brass hexies, and the movement and contrast within the final design is just unexpected enough to draw the eye.

▼ **YOU'LL NEED**

Pliers

Soft Flex wire

Tape

Nine angular double-drilled metal hexagon frame beads measuring ¾ in. across

Eleven 4-mm green glass cubes for movement

Two crimp beads

Magnetic clasp

FINISHED SIZE

7 in.

1. Cut a 12-in. piece of Soft Flex wire and double a piece of tape at one end. Add a single contrast bead, then add the first hexagon bead, passing the Soft Flex wire through one side's hole, adding an inner cube bead, and then passing the wire through the second side's hole, so the cube is neatly inside the metal frame.

2. Continue stringing frame beads with contrast beads inside each one until you've reached the length you want for the bracelet. Add a final contrast bead to the end.

3. Add a crimp bead and then one half of a magnetic clasp. Pass the Soft Flex wire back through the crimp bead and the first contrast bead, pulling it taut, and use flat-nose pliers to crimp the bead securely. Trim the beading wire tail.

4. Take the tape off the side you started with and repeat step 3 to add a crimp bead and the other half of the magnetic clasp there.

Tip: To choose contrast beads for your piece, lay the angular metal shapes out in a row and look for small beads that fit easily within the negative space. I auditioned 6-mm glass cubes but realized they'd barely have any space to move freely within the design, so I chose smaller 4-mm cubes for my final bracelet.

Design Principles: Negative Space

This is a very simple but impactful factor in our jewelry: what isn't there within an overall design. Consider giving the piece some room to breathe. You can include intriguing negative space by using filigree, loops, circles, or other beads or components with open areas, or by using unadorned chain to suspend an elaborate or detailed pendant or earring.

My Favorite Bracelets

▶ **TECHNIQUES:**

Gluing Rainbow Button Bracelet, Button Box Bracelet / **Jump Rings** Charm Bangle Bracelet

All three of these bracelets have that intangible quality of joyfulness when you put them on. They aren't themed in any certain way, and they don't use particularly similar colors or materials, but they all remind me of what I love most about handmade jewelry: how personal, fun, and full of life it can be.

Rainbow Button Bracelet

● ○ ○ **EASY**

This bracelet was inspired by my rainbow-loving six-year-old daughter, Pearl. We looked for buttons in just the right size, one for each ROYGBIV color, in my collection and then hit the fabric store together to track down the last few (who knew orange was such a challenge to find?). In one bit of artistic license, you'll see that we switched out indigo for a cheerful pink. In first grade, just about everything needs a little pink, and bracelets are no exception.

Tip: This project is very kid-friendly in terms of design, but the strong glue is only to be used by adults in a workspace with good ventilation. Nontoxic craft glues likely won't hold the buttons down securely enough, so let kids choose the button placement and order, and then delegate the gluing part of the project to a grown-up.

▼ YOU'LL NEED

Link bracelet (I used one with seven links, each with a round recessed setting perfect for buttons, but you could use a flat-linked style)

Seven sew-through buttons of rainbow color order, or another color palette

Strong glue

FINISHED SIZE

7 in.

1. Decide on the button color order. Pearl and I chose a modified version of rainbow colors from left to right.

2. Apply a generous dab of glue into the recessed setting of each link (or if you are using a flat style, onto the center of each link). Press each button down to join them. Let the bracelet dry completely before wearing.

Button Box Bracelet

● ● ○ **INTERMEDIATE**

I absolutely love covered buttons, and this simple project spotlights fabric in clean, simple circles that decorate a bracelet. You can make your own version in any size or scale of covered buttons. Make a matching pendant on p. 111.

▼ YOU'LL NEED

Pliers

One bracelet blank (I purchased mine at www.eloxite.com)

Covered-button kit with five to six ¾-in. buttons

Fabric remnant of your choice

Sharp scissors

Glue (I used Aleene's Platinum Bond 7800®)

Five or six plain sew-through buttons smaller than the covered buttons

FINISHED SIZE

7 in.

1. Following the covered-button kit package directions and template, cut out the fabric circles for the buttons. I cut six of the same fabric for one bracelet and mixed two complementary fabrics for the other—four of one print and a single contrast of the other just for fun.

2. Before making the covered buttons, use pliers to remove the shank from each button backing. (You can also remove it after the buttons are finished, but I think it's easier to do it first.)

3. Create five or six covered buttons (or the number needed to make a bracelet, one for each link), following the package directions.

4. Apply a generous dab of glue right into the back of the first covered button and press a plain sew-through button into it. Repeat with the other covered buttons. Let them set until the glue is mostly or completely dry and the inner button is not easily moved.

5. Once the glue is set, use another generous dab of glue to attach one covered button to each link of the bracelet. Let the glue set completely before wearing.

Tip: For these covered-button projects, I recommend a multidirectional or nondirectional print with small enough details to capture, like the Denyse Schmidt print shown at left in chocolate brown and white. I loved using a couple of my favorite Cotton+Steel fabrics with metallic color prints—they look beautiful as jewelry!

Charm Bangle Bracelet

 ○ ○ **EASY**

A sleek metal bangle is the perfect setting for a beautiful set of charms that speaks to you. I found several types of bangles at large craft stores and really liked this doubled loop style with a hook clasp. The charms are neatly contained in one quadrant of the overall circle but still have plenty of movement. This would also work nicely on a simple slip-on bangle with no restrictions.

▼ YOU'LL NEED

Pliers

Plain metal bangle of your choice

A handful of favorite charms (I used five)

4-mm jump rings for each charm (I used seven, since two of my charms were dual-ring styles)

FINISHED SIZE

6½ in.

1. Lay the charms out in an order that appeals to you. I mixed one- and two-ring charms with smaller ones at each side and more substantial ones in the middle area.

2. Open the jump rings, one (or two) per charm, and begin attaching the charms to the bangle, working left to right. For dual-ring charms, like my horseshoe and lovebirds, be sure to allow enough space for them to move freely rather than feel jammed together or overcrowded.

Vintage Gone Modern Bracelets

▶ **TECHNIQUES: Jump Rings** Sparkle Bangle Bracelet, Sparkle Flowers Bracelet / **Gluing** Sparkle Flowers Bracelet / **Wrapped Loops** Sparkle & Shine Bracelet

These vintage-inspired bracelets are all about the sparkle. Whether they feature family heirloom crystal beads wire wrapped into a delicate chain, a lovely set of vintage Lucite flowers with tiny rhinestone centers sparkling away, or an ultra-simple embellished bangle with teardrops that clink together, these are the perfect pieces to wear somewhere special. ❧

Sparkle & Shine Bracelet

❀ ❀ ❀ **INTERMEDIATE**

I used some of the round and bicone crystal beads saved from my great-aunt Sue's broken jewelry to make this simple, lovely bracelet. You can see these same beads in my Vintage Sparkles Necklace (see pp. 73–74) and the Three-Generation Pendant (see p. 97) I made for my mother. Use any special sparkly beads for this project, whether they're three-generations-ago family pieces like mine or something beautiful that caught your eye at the bead store this morning.

▼ **YOU'LL NEED**

Pliers
24-gauge sterling wire
Five sparkly 8-mm round beads
Five sparkly 9-mm bicone beads
Magnetic clasp

FINISHED SIZE

6½ in.

1. Cut ten 4-in. pieces of wire, one for each of the beads. Add a wrapped loop on one side of the first piece of wire to transform it into a bead connector. Add a wrapped loop to the opposite side, but do not complete the wrap yet. Slip one half of the magnetic clasp into the loop, and then complete the wrap to join it securely. You will now have the first bead joined to the clasp to start the bracelet.

2. Repeat with the second bead, alternating round and bicone beads and joining the second connector to the first one before completing the wrapped loop, just as you did in step 1. You now have two beads joined with a clasp at one end.

3. Continue adding beads to the bracelet one by one, working left to right. Try the bracelet on or measure it to check its length. When it is the length you want, add the other half of the magnetic clasp to the open end of the last bead and complete the wrap to join them securely.

Sparkle Bangle Bracelet

❀ ❀ ❀ **EASY**

Like the Charm Bangle Bracelet (see p. 157), this ultra-simple design adds a few thoughtful embellishments to a plain bangle, giving it a life and shine that make it a joy to wear. I added just three identical teardrop sparkle charms to my bracelet, but you can mix in as many as you like, matching or assorted, for your own vintage-inspired piece.

▼ **YOU'LL NEED**

Pliers
Plain metal bangle of your choice
Three sparkly teardrop charms or other charms you love
Three 4-mm or larger jump rings for each charm

FINISHED SIZE

7 in.

1. Lay the sparkle charms out flat and open the jump rings, one per charm.

2. Begin attaching the charms to the bangle, working left to right. Be sure to allow enough space for them to move freely rather than feel jammed together or overcrowded.

Sparkle Flowers Bracelet

🌷 🌷 🌷 **EASY**

This bracelet is a distant cousin to the Button Blossoms Bracelet (see p. 147), reinterpreting the same idea of adding pretty flat-backed flowers to a bracelet blank. However, changing the materials, scale, color palette, and feel lends this little piece a vintage charm that's all its own. The components you choose can be as bold or as delicate as you like, but don't forget the sparkle!

▼ **YOU'LL NEED**

Pliers

Bracelet blank or 7-in. length of flat circle chain

10 flat-backed vintage flower cabochons, one per link (I used nine coral and one aqua for pop)

10 rhinestones (one per flower)

Strong glue

Magnetic clasp plus two 4-mm jump rings

FINISHED SIZE

7 in.

1. Glue one flower cabochon to each link of the bracelet. I chose to place my single offbeat-color flower close to one end of the bracelet to draw the eye.

2. Carefully glue a small rhinestone sparkle onto the center of each flower. Let it dry completely before moving the bracelet.

3. Add one half of a magnetic clasp to each end of the bracelet using 4-mm jump rings.

Tip: Choose flowers or other vintage cabochons you love with flat backs, lightweight enough to wear in multiples on your wrist.

Tip: Find a bracelet blank or wide, substantial flat chain you can glue these flowers onto. I used a flat circle chain with thick, sturdy links above the flat, recessed circles for an interesting effect, but a premade bracelet would work beautifully, too.

Botanical Décor

▶ **TECHNIQUES:**
Plain Loops Tassels on Chain, Beaded Vase Necklace / **Jump Rings** All / **Briolette Wrapping** Circle & Briolette Drop Chain

I collect ceramic bowls and vases, and thought I'd add some beaded embellishments to a few of my favorite pieces. This simple project works well with any narrow or curved jar or vase that allows the necklace-style decoration to sit in place. Take your design cues from the colors, shapes, and styles of the pieces you're working with.

Tassels on Chain

 ● ● ○ **INTERMEDIATE**

I made a miniaturized version of my suede tassels from the Earth Tone Tassel Earrings (see p. 39) by simply trimming the fringe to a narrower size before winding it up. Mixing organic carnelian beads with antiqued circle chain and those soft tassels added something special to one of my favorite ceramic vases.

▼ YOU'LL NEED

Vase

Pliers

20-gauge wire

Chain of your choice (I used 7 in. of circle chain)

One 4-mm jump ring

Two eyepins

7-in.-wide piece of suede fringe, trimmed to 1¼ in. long

Two beads of your choice (I used organic carnelians that measured about ¾ in. long)

Scissors

Glue

FINISHED SIZE

12 in.

1. Measure the narrowest part of the vase's neck. Cut a piece of chain at least twice that long, so that the two ends will extend below the join. My vase was about 3½ in. around, so I cut my chain to 7 in. long. You can cut a longer piece if you're using a taller elongated vase or want a more dramatic embellishment.

2. Drape the chain around the neck of the vase and connect two links using a jump ring (as shown in the photo) so it hangs nicely. Just eye this; there's no need to measure exactly. I chose to offset my chain so that the two ends were different lengths—one two links and one three links long.

3. Once you're happy with the chain arrangement, cut two 3-in. pieces of 20-gauge wire and turn the beads into connectors with plain loops on either side. Connect each of them to one end of chain.

4. To create tassels, trim fringe to 1¼ in. from top to bottom. Cut two 3½-in. lengths and set them flat on your worksurface. Place an eyepin at one end of the first fringe piece, with the round "eye" surfacing just above the top edge, and add glue. Begin rolling the fringe into a spiral so that the eyepin is tucked neatly inside the center, adding dabs of glue as you roll the fringe. Finish by carefully gluing the far end of the fringe down, making sure that the tassel is symmetrical and neat and the fringe is smooth. The loop of the eyepin should be centered above the tassel for hanging.

5. Repeat step 4 to make the other tassel with the second piece of fringe and eyepin. Carefully open the loops to join the tassels to the beads.

Circle & Briolette Drop Chain

 ● ● ○ **INTERMEDIATE**

For a swimming-pool-blue vase I found in California, I wanted to add a mix of metals and colors with a pendant-style embellishment. I chose another decorative chain I love (left over from my Leaves on Chain Bracelet project on p. 146) and added a circular frame with a faceted glass briolette drop in the center.

▼ YOU'LL NEED

Vase

Pliers

Decorative chain (I used 6 in.)

One 4-mm jump ring

Circular or other framing piece

One briolette drilled side to side

20-gauge wire

FINISHED SIZE

8 in.

1. Measure the part of the vase's neck where you'd like the embellishment to hang. Cut a piece of chain that long, so that the two ends will join in the center. Mine was about 6 in. around, which included room for the framing piece to hang in a V-shape at the front.

(Continued)

2. Drape the chain around the neck of the vase and connect the outer two links using a jump ring so it hangs nicely.

3. Create the pendant embellishment by creating a simplified hanger-style wire connector for the briolette, passing the upper loop through the circle's hole before completing it. (See "Briolette wrapping" on p. 25 for more detailed instructions.)

4. Open the jump ring that connects the chain ends and carefully slip the briolette pendant on. Close the jump ring securely.

Beaded Vase Necklace

 EASY

This project is a nice way to use over-size seed beads or other small pieces harmoniously, with an optional embellishment in front. I kept my color palette very simple and very limited, taking my cues from the organic earth tones of the vase glaze.

▼ YOU'LL NEED

Vase

Pliers

20-gauge wire

Two different small beads (I used a total of 16 round translucent amber beads [A], and eight organic-shaped opaque gold/brown beads [B])

One 6-mm jump ring

Pendant embellishment (optional; I used a wooden piece with a slight teardrop shape)

FINISHED SIZE

8 in.

1. Measure the part of the vase's neck where you want the beaded "necklace" to sit. Mine was about 6 in. around. Cut eight 3-in. pieces of 20-gauge wire (or one for each of the bead links you'll be using) and form plain loops at the end of each one.

2. Place the beads you're using on the first piece of wire in a pattern you like. I chose A-B-A. Form a plain loop on the other side to make the row of beads into a connector.

3. Repeat step 2 to make seven more bead connectors the same way. Open the plain loops to join the connectors into a chain, and link the two ends the same way to make a closed circle of beaded chain. Place it on the vase.

4. If you'd like to add a pendant piece, open the 6-mm jump ring, pass it through one of the bead chain links, and slip the pendant onto it. Close it securely so that the pendant hangs facing forward.

Pretty Jars

▶ **TECHNIQUES:**

   Gluing All / **Painting** All

I use glass jars for storage all over my house, but they're especially handy for beads and buttons. I came up with a few ways to decorate and personalize the ones I reach for every day. Paint, glaze, or embellish yours the way you like best! This is a super-simple and very customizable project.

Sparkle Flower Jars

● ○ ○ **EASY**

I loved the way a simple pint jar looked painted with opaque, creamy blue and thought I'd try something similar with a small vase and a deep glossy orange color. Adding sparkly rhinestone flowers to each one in the same spot gave the two vessels a nice relationship.

▼ **YOU'LL NEED**

Plain glass jars or vases

Glass paint

Paintbrush

Glue

Rhinestones (I used six oval/ marquise shapes for my petals and one round for my center)

FINISHED SIZE

Varies

1. Paint the jar or vase with at least two coats of glass paint, letting it dry completely between coats. You can see that I painted my larger jar on the *outside* for a creamy, opaque appearance and painted my smaller, square vase on the *inside* for a glossy, shiny appearance. It's up to you how you approach yours. I also painted my jar lid with the same glass paint and let that dry separately, too.

2. When you're happy with the paint coverage, design a little flower embellishment using flat-backed rhinestones. I placed six marquise rhinestones in a circular formation like flower petals, then put the center round over the middle area.

3. Decide on the flower placement on the jar (I chose the lower right-hand corner on both my jar and my vase) and lay it down flat. Working with one petal at a time, carefully glue them into place. I glued one petal down, then glued its counterpart directly across so that the flower grew symmetrically. Glue the flower center over the middle area where the petals meet.

Tip: Choose glass jars with flat sides, if possible.

Embellished Label Jars

● ○ ○ **EASY**

This ultra-simple label embellishment is a fun way to keep your beads or buttons organized. Paint your jar with colorful translucent glaze, or keep the glass clear if you'd prefer. You can either find pre-made labels and paper flowers at a craft store or make your own custom versions.

▼ **YOU'LL NEED**

Plain glass jars

Sheer glass paint (optional)

Labels

Glue stick (optional)

Paper flowers

Flat-backed rhinestones (one per paper flower)

Craft glue

FINISHED SIZE

Varies

1. Decide if you want to paint the jars with translucent glaze-style glass paint. If you do want to add color, follow the package directions to apply glaze to the inside of the jars, swirl it evenly, and let it dry, removing the excess. You should have a clear view of the jar's contents while adding a pop of interesting color.

2. Make your own labels or choose nice premade labels at a craft store. Type or write the jar contents on them, and apply them to the side of the jar with their own adhesive or a glue stick.

3. Make or buy pretty paper flowers and glue a single rhinestone to the center of each one, letting it dry completely. Glue the flowers to the upper corner of each label for decoration.

Bead & Button Jars

● ○ ○ EASY

Why not decorate a plain glass jar with something pretty, especially if you can see what's inside? I made a set of a quart-size button jar, a pint-size bead jar, and a wide half-pint-size embellishment jar for my craft room, and I loved the results. You can find colorful jars or use clear ones, but it's much easier to embellish a flat-sided jar than a curved, round one.

▼ YOU'LL NEED

Jars with flat sides

Rhinestones, sew-through buttons, flat-backed flowers, or other embellishments

Silicone glue

FINISHED SIZE

Varies

1. Improvise a simple design using buttons, rhinestones, flowers, or other embellishments on a flat surface. You can see my button jar's flowers were made by pairing two different sizes of the same round vintage sew-through buttons with small marquise rhinestone "leaves." My bead jar's repeating design was made with two sizes of round rhinestones, and my embellishment jar was simply decorated with paper flowers with rhinestone centers.

2. Once you're happy with your design, place the jar on its side. Lift the decorations one at a time and glue them down with silicone glue, pressing them in place. Let the glue dry while the jar is still on its side so the pieces don't slide.

3. Let the glue dry completely before using the jar. Fill it with pretty materials that relate to the decorations, or make a simple tag that describes the contents, especially if you're giving it as a gift.

Holiday Sparkle

▶ **TECHNIQUES:**

Gluing All / **Painting** Star Shadow Box Ornament

These three holiday ornaments all draw inspiration from vintage pieces I've found, from bottlebrush trees and 1960s postage stamps to spun-cotton mushrooms. Choose your own favorites to design around, or fall in love with something new.

Vintage Stamp Ornaments

● ○ ○ **EASY**

I love old postage stamps and found a little handful of Christmas stamps I thought would be pretty ornaments behind glass. Here are two of my favorites.

▼ **YOU'LL NEED**

Postage stamps

Glass squares or rectangles (mine measured 1 in. by 1 in. and 1 in. by 2 in.)

JudiKins Diamond Glaze or other glass/paper glue

Washi tape (optional)

Acid-free cardstock

Scissors

Pencil

Pendant bail

Strong glue

Ornament hanger or 20-gauge wire and pliers

FINISHED SIZE

1¼ in.

1. Choose your stamps and find glass squares or rectangles that fit over them nicely to frame and magnify them. For a smaller square stamp, I found a 1-in. square worked very well, and for a wider rectangle stamp, I used a 1-in. by 2-in. glass piece with some extra space at either side.

2. Use a pencil to trace the glass squares or rectangles on cardstock and cut out the shapes for backing. Trim away any excess that shows around the glass. If you have sections showing around the stamp (like my rectangular ornament), you can cover the cardstock with neat strips of washi tape as a backdrop.

3. Glue the stamp to the backing using paper glue and let it set. Apply more glue over the stamp surface and press the glass piece over it. Allow it to dry completely.

4. Glue a small pendant bail at the upper center of each ornament using strong glue. Let it dry completely, then add an ornament hanger. To make your own version, as I did, cut a 4-in. piece of 20-gauge wire and make a wrapped loop at one end, slipping the pendant bail loop into it before completing the wrap. Use your fingers to gently curve the wire end to form a hanger shape, trimming it to size.

Tiny Tree Terrarium

● ○ ○ **EASY**

I love bottlebrush trees and was so excited to find a pack of teeny-tiny ones at the craft store. I found a small jar that turned my little tree into a terrarium-style mantel decoration, complete with pearl-white bead "snow" and hot pink ornaments.

▼ YOU'LL NEED

Tiny bottlebrush tree (mine measured about 1⅛ in. tall)

Small glass jar with cork stopper that the tree fits into easily (mine measured 1¾ in. tall and about 3 in. around)

Glue

Colorful oversize seed beads to use as ornaments

Small white seed beads

Tiny eyepin screw (optional)

Ornament hanger (optional)

FINISHED SIZE

2 in.

1. Test your small jar size by carefully placing the tree inside. You'll want to be able to close the jar with the cork stopper easily, but the tree itself won't need tons of space all around. Remove the tree and get ready to embellish it.

2. Using small dabs of glue, place colorful beads in different places on the tree. I used eight on my tree, so each side was decorated. Let them dry completely.

3. Open the jar and add a generous amount of glue inside, so it covers the bottom of the jar. Try not to get any glue on the sides of the jar. Carefully lower the beaded tree into the jar, and press it into the glue so it's centered and level.

4. Pour a small amount of pearly white seed beads into the jar for "snow," shaking and swirling the jar gently so they settle over the glue at the bottom, surrounding the base of the tree. Let the glue dry completely, then shake out any excess beads.

5. If you want to hang your ornament from the tree, twist a tiny eyepin-style screw from the hardware store into the top of the cork topper and slip an ornament hanger into it. Or, display the tree terrarium on your mantel or table instead.

Star Shadow Box Ornament

● ● ○ **INTERMEDIATE**

I found this star shadow box as a kit at the craft store, but you can use any small matchbox or other open-front box you have instead. I painted mine and glued on sequins, while adding a backdrop of fabric, but you can finish yours, and add whatever focal pieces, as you like.

▼ **YOU'LL NEED**

Shadow box or other open-fronted box (mine measured 2¼ in. across)

Gold paint

Paintbrush

Washi tape or fabric

Glue

Sequins

Focal piece (I used a square aqua rhinestone)

Small eyepin screw (optional)

Ornament hanger (optional)

FINISHED SIZE

Length: 2½ in.

1. Use the paintbrush to paint the shadow box with two coats of gold paint.

2. Line the inside of the shadow box with fabric, washi tape, or any other decoration. (I used washi tape patterned with jewels in metallic colors.)

3. Glue something interesting inside the shadow box. I glued down an aqua rhinestone. If you purchased an unassembled shadow box, build it now.

4. If you want to hang your shadow box, twist a tiny eyepin-style screw from the hardware store into the top of the shadow box and slip an ornament hanger into it (see the Vintage Stamp Ornaments on p. 169 for details).

Tip: My shadow box came unassembled, and I built it after decorating it, but you can also embellish a premade shadow box.

Little Gifts

▶ **TECHNIQUES:**

Jump Rings Quick Bookmark / **Wrapped Loops** Quick Bookmark /
Painting Trio of Buttons Picture Frame / **Gluing** Geometric Magnets,
Trio of Buttons Picture Frame

 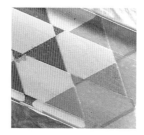 

These three projects are easy and fast to make and fun to give as gifts to friends, teachers, family, or anyone else special. Choose bright colors and designs that suit the recipient nicely, or keep one for yourself!

1. Trace the glass square or rectangle onto acid-free cardstock with a pencil. Apply strips of washi tape over the traced shape, lining them up neatly so the edges are harmonious. I used one washi tape design on my smaller magnet and alternated two on my larger one. (Note: If you use decorative paper or another image, trace the glass piece over it the same way you did on the cardstock, capturing any details you like best, and cut it out. Glue it onto the cardstock.)

2. Cut out the cardstock shape and trim away any edges that show around the glass piece. Glue the cardstock to the back of the glass shape using Diamond Glaze. Let it dry completely.

3. Apply a generous dab of strong glue to the back of each glass piece. Press a magnet into each one.

Quick Bookmark

● ○ ○ **EASY**

This gift is as pretty as it is practical. Find a metal bookmark with a ring on the end, add a mix of fun beads or a special charm, and it's just the thing for a book lover to keep on the nightstand.

 YOU'LL NEED

Pliers

Blank metal bookmark with ring (available at many bead stores)

Beads with headpins or charms with jump rings (I used blue and orange Lucite)

FINISHED SIZE

6 in.

1. If you're using beads, put each bead on a headpin and form the first half of a wrapped loop. If you're using charms, open each charm's jump ring.

2. Place the beads or charms on the bookmark ring in the order you want them to hang. Close the jump rings or complete the wrapped loops.

Geometric Magnets

● ○ ○ **EASY**

Like the Washi Tape Triangles Pendant (see p. 110), these simple magnets are eye-catching and fun, but also practical —who couldn't use a few more refrigerator magnets? I applied strips of washi tape to create my background design, but you can also use any decorative paper you like.

▼ **YOU'LL NEED**

Glass squares or rectangles (mine measured 1 in. across, and 1 in. by 2 in.)

Washi tape, decorative paper, or another interesting, colorful background

JudiKins Diamond Glaze or other glass/paper glue

Strong glue

Acid-free cardstock

Pencil

Scissors

Magnets

Trio of Buttons Picture Frame

● ○ ○ **EASY**

I found this unfinished pine picture frame at the craft store and knew it would be a lot of fun to decorate. I painted it a smooth and even gold and then chose a favorite photo of me and my two-and-a-half-year-old daughter just a few weeks before my son was born. Surprise someone special with a favorite photo in this personalized frame. This one is going in my daughter's room, as a reminder of those last precious weeks of waiting to meet her little brother.

▼ **YOU'LL NEED**

Unfinished wood picture frame

Favorite photo

Paint

Paintbrush

Washi tape

Hot glue and glue gun

Vintage buttons or other elements

FINISHED SIZE

7½ in. square

1. Paint the picture frame in a base color you love. I chose gold, which brings out warm tones beautifully.

2. Decide how to decorate the frame. I took my embellishment inspiration from the yellows, reds, and blues in the picture by using a neat strip of the same washi tape from my Geometric Magnets (see p. 173) anchored by a trio of blue vintage buttons left over from my wool Ribbon Rosette Clip

(see p. 122), along with three yellow buttons from my Button Blossoms Bracelet (see p. 147) nestled in their centers.

3. Once you've chosen your decorative elements, apply them in layers. I added a horizontal strip of washi tape below the photo, then placed my buttons in a trio at the lower right corner. Glue the buttons in place, lifting them one at a time so they stay in formation.

Tip: It's best to choose a favorite photograph to frame and then find an unfinished wood picture frame in the correct size.

Design Principles: Graphic and Linear

These bold patterns are brought to life in jewelry, clothing, embellishments, and any other design and draw inspiration from basic geometry. In the Picture Frame (above) you can see how the clean horizontal line of the washi tape adds visual weight to the bottom of the frame to anchor it in place, while also being offset by the circular buttons.

My Favorite Embellishments

▶ **TECHNIQUES:**

Wrapped Loop Lovebirds Handbag Charm / **Gluing** Charming Corsages, Rhinestone Clip

These three pieces just make me happy. I love the simplicity and beautiful colors of the bright lovebirds charm, the sparkly rhinestone clip is perfect for my long hair, and the exuberant little floral corsage brooches are some of my favorite things to wear, ever. I hope you find inspiration in this book to make some of your own all-time favorites, too!

Rhinestone Clip

● ○ ○ **EASY**

I almost never wore this simple rhinestone barrette until I embellished it with a little something special—a filigree flower like the ones I used in my Button Blossoms Bracelet (see p. 147), punctuated by a sparkling faceted rhinestone center. A 30-second craft pick-me-up brought this piece to life. It's certainly not an intricate upgrade, but let's face it: Sometimes simple is best!

▼ **YOU'LL NEED**

**Plain or flat-topped barrette
    or hair clip**
Filigree flower charm
Rhinestone
Strong glue

FINISHED SIZE

3 in.

1. Lay out the filigree flower and rhinestone and decide where they would sit nicely on the barrette. I chose to place mine near the end, about ⅓ in. from the edge.

2. Apply a generous dab of strong glue at your chosen spot and press the flower into it. Add a small dab of glue in the center and press the rhinestone into the flower. Let dry completely.

Lovebirds Handbag Charm

● ○ ○ **EASY**

Any oversize colorful charm or embellishment you love would be fun to spotlight in this simple project. I found my lovebirds at Dava Bead & Trade in Portland, Oregon (see Resources, p. 184) and paired them with a brick-red vintage bead that made the aqua even brighter. Use it to decorate a handbag, as a keychain, or wherever it fits best!

▼ **YOU'LL NEED**

Pliers
**Large charm or decorative
    element you love**
Contrast bead
20-gauge wire
Keychain-style loop/hanger

FINISHED SIZE

4 in.

1. Cut a 5-in. piece of 20-gauge craft wire and form the first half of a generously sized wrapped loop at one end. Put the charm on the loop, right at the top of the design, and complete the wrap to close it securely.

2. Place the contrast bead on the wire and form the first half of a wrapped loop on the other side. Slip the keychain into place on the loop and complete the wrap.

Charming Corsages

● ● ○ **INTERMEDIATE**

Craft-store floral sprays are some of my favorite secret ingredients for beautiful jewelry and embellishment projects, like the Winter Pearls Necklace (see pp. 74–75), the Winter Pearls Hair Comb (see p. 125), and these adorable corsages. They're so easy to make that you'll want to put them together in all your favorite color combinations. Have a corsage-making party with friends—you can make lots of them from the same few colorful sprays of silk flowers.

▼ **YOU'LL NEED**

Assorted floral sprays (you can often make more than one corsage out of a single spray)

Embellishments (I used a butterfly and a vintage rhinestone setting)

Pliers

24-gauge craft wire or floral wire

Hot glue and glue gun

Floral tape

Pin backs (one per corsage)

FINISHED SIZE

5 in. to 6 in.

1. Choose three to five small floral spray sections from larger branches. You can either use multiples of the same style of silk flowers (like my orange and gold version) or mix several (like my pink one). Arrange them together in an appealing way. I like to hold the stems closely and let the flowers fan out naturally above, with two or three sections of leaves at the back of the flower design.

2. Wrap floral or craft wire around the stems to hold them in place. Wire or hot-glue the embellishment in place. Wrap the wire tightly and trim the end so it's flush with or tucked into the corsage.

3. Wrap the base of the corsage tightly with floral tape, moving from top to bottom and back again. Open the pin back and place it on the back, oriented vertically, then tape over the spine of it several more times to hold it securely in place.

4. If you'd like, cover the floral tape stem in tulle, fabric, lace, or any other decorative element.

Tip: I like to mix a few different elements into each of my corsages, starting with one to three different floral spray stems. I add leaves and greenery behind them to frame the center design, and I finish the whole corsage off with a little ornament, like a broken rhinestone setting or a vintage butterfly. Experiment with different combinations until you find your corsage inspiration!

Vintage Gone Modern Embellishments

▶ **TECHNIQUES: Gluing** Sparkle Flowers Handbag, Sequin Flowers Handbag **/**
Stitching Three Rings Handbag

Vintage handbags are attractive, but sometimes the black or brown ones can be especially plain in their finish. Adding sparkle or metallic elements can give these beautiful but sedate bags a new lease on life. ❧

Sparkle Flowers Handbag

 INTERMEDIATE

If you have a plain patent-leather handbag lying around that could use a little pick-me-up, how about embellishing it with a fun, sparkly design? I used a handful of colored rhinestones to create a flower pattern on the front of my purse in the style of Enid Collins, one of my favorite vintage designers. Follow these directions to make a floral arrangement or create your own design with other shapes, sizes, and colors. Look for rhinestones at specialty bead stores or larger craft stores like Michaels®.

▼ YOU'LL NEED

Plain vintage or new patent-leather or hard-sided handbag

Craft glue of your choice (I recommend Aleene's Original Tacky Glue or Jewel-It Embellishing Glue)

Toothpicks for spreading glue (optional)

Three round rhinestones for flower centers (I used small, medium, and large)

15 oval or marquise rhinestones in the same color as flower centers for border

25 oval or marquise rhinestones in a contrast color for petals

FINISHED SIZE

Varies

1. Place the flower centers on the bag in the desired spots. I arranged mine so that the small and medium-size centers were on the left half in a loose diagonal, and the large one was centered on the right half.

2. Glue the flower centers down securely with craft glue. I used Aleene's Jewel-It Embellishing Glue for these larger rounds. If any glue peeks out around the edges, you can wait for it to partially set and then use a toothpick or tweezers to pull it away.

3. Use a toothpick to dab Aleene's Original Tacky Glue onto the back of a contrasting-color rhinestone. Starting with the largest flower center, press the petal rhinestone down above the flower center, applying it to the purse. Repeat, adding a second petal at the bottom of the flower center.

4. Add a second set of petals to the same flower center next to each of the first petals, spacing them slightly apart, as shown. Continue adding petals all the way around until you have used a total of 10 petal rhinestones.

5. Begin adding petals to the small flower center by gluing one petal at the top and two at the bottom instead of just one (as shown in the photo on the facing page). This asymmetrical style is to accommodate an odd number of petals. Fill in the sides of the second flower with four more petals as shown in the photo, eyeing them instead of arranging them symmetrically, until you have used a total of seven rhinestones.

6. Begin adding petals to the medium-size flower center and arrange the petals symmetrically just as you did for the large flower center in steps 3 and 4. Continue adding rhinestones until you have a total of eight petals.

7. Begin the simple decorative border by gluing the rhinestones that match the flower centers in straight lines until you have covered the front of the purse from side to side and top to bottom, or as desired. Let the purse dry overnight.

Three Rings Handbag

 **EASY**

This brown velvet clutch was ornamented with a small gold clasp but not much else to draw the eye. I found three textured gold oval rings and thought they'd look nice in the center of such a simple bag—and now I carry it all the time! Add your own favorites to yours. As a bonus, you can easily remove any of these hand-stitched designs if you want to change things around later!

▼ YOU'LL NEED

Plain handbag with fabric sides
Three oval rings (mine measured 1 in. by 1½ in.) or other embellishments
Needle and invisible thread
Scissors

FINISHED SIZE

Varies

1. Choose and lay out the embellishments. I put my ovals in a neat horizontal line at the center of my bag.

2. Guide the lining out of the bag so it's not caught in your hand-stitching. Thread a needle with invisible thread. Working from one side to the other, begin stitching down the ovals, making at least three careful stitches on each horizontal side of the ovals. Bring the needle up from the back to advance to the next spot you're stitching, so the thread is hidden.

3. Once you've sewn the last area of the three ovals down, knot securely and hide the thread behind the last oval.

Sequin Flowers Handbag

 **EASY**

Like the Three Rings Handbag (see the facing page), this black satin purse was utterly plain except for the gold clasp. I found vintage flower sequins in the same rich gold and added tiny black rhinestones over their centers to tie the embellishments together.

▼ **YOU'LL NEED**

Plain handbag with relatively smooth fabric or flat sides

Three sequins

Three small rhinestones

Strong glue

Toothpick

FINISHED SIZE

Varies

1. Choose and lay out the embellishments. I put my flower sequins in a small triangle pattern at the lower right-hand corner of my bag.

2. Glue the embellishments down securely. Using a toothpick, add a tiny dab of glue at the center of each sequin and place a small rhinestone there. Let the glue dry completely before using the bag.

METRIC EQUIVALENTS

One inch equals approximately 2.54 centimeters. To convert inches to centimeters, multiply the figure in inches by 2.54 and round off to the nearest half centimeter, or use the chart below, whose figures are rounded off (1 centimeter equals 10 millimeters).

1/8 in.	= 3 mm		9 in.	= 23 cm
1/4 in.	= 6 mm		10 in.	= 25.5 cm
3/8 in.	= 1 cm		12 in.	= 30.5 cm
1/2 in.	= 1.3 cm		14 in.	= 35.5 cm
5/8 in.	= 1.5 cm		15 in.	= 38 cm
3/4 in.	= 2 cm		16 in.	= 40.5 cm
7/8 in.	= 2.2 cm		18 in.	= 45.5 cm
1 in.	= 2.5 cm		20 in.	= 51 cm
2 in.	= 5 cm		21 in.	= 53.5 cm
3 in.	= 7.5 cm		22 in.	= 56 cm
4 in.	= 10 cm		24 in.	= 61 cm
5 in.	= 12.5 cm		25 in.	= 63.5 cm
6 in.	= 15 cm		36 in.	= 92 cm
7 in.	= 18 cm		45 in.	= 114.5 cm
8 in.	= 20.5 cm		60 in.	= 152 cm

Christina Batch-Lee is an artist and jewelry designer in Brooklyn, New York. Her jewelry line, Missbatch, features rough-cut natural gemstones and vintage metal accents and findings and can be found at some choice Brooklyn boutiques and at Missbatch.etsy.com. She works to share her love of creativity and all things DIY while teaching art and craft classes at www.BrooklynCraftCompany.com.

Michelle Freedman started making jewelry in her family's garage at age 10. She studied fashion design in college, and these days she sews and draws daily in her adopted hometown of Portland, Oregon. She's contributed to several of Susan Beal's books, including *Hand-Stitched Home* and *Sewing for All Seasons,* and she designs projects for magazines like *Stitch, Generation Q,* and *McCall's.* Read about her creative endeavors on her blog, www.designcamppdx.blogspot.com.

Alexis Hartman is a fine artist and the illustrator of many craft books, including Susan Beal's *Bead Simple* and *Button It Up.* She also designs the evocative nature-inspired Lake August line of textiles and wallpapers. She lives in Los Angeles with her husband, Andrew, and their son, Hugo. See more of her work at www.lakeaugust.com.

Lynzee Lynx Malsin is a wild-child creative, working in many mediums. With a love for color, form, and meaning, she creates jewelry, paintings, clothing, and worlds. She is at work in her Portland, Oregon, studio putting together an e-course on applying the art process to make life and world changes. Find her jewelry, paintings, and writing online: www.lynzeelynx.com and www.lynzeelynx.etsy.com.

Torie Nguyen designs and crafts a line of jewelry called Totinette bijoux. She draws inspiration from her love of art, color, old jazz music, architecture, vintage glamour, and her daughter, Matilda. She is also the co-owner of Crafty Wonderland (www.craftywonderland.com), a retail store and biannual craft market in Portland, Oregon.

Kayte Terry is an artist and the author of three craft books, including the best-selling *Paper Made!,* and has contributed her DIYs to numerous books and blogs. Kayte recently left a decade-long career on the visual team at Anthropologie to pursue her MFA in Fine Art. It's the best decision she's ever made, so far. Kayte lives in Philadelphia with her husband, Adam, and their two, one-eyed cats, Odin and Poundcake.

Cathy Zwicker is a mom, artist, and entrepreneur living in southeast Portland, Oregon, with her two favorite humans and her two favorite cats. She is co-founder and organizer of Crafty Wonderland, a twice-yearly art and craft market and retail shop selling handmade goods. Cathy is inspired by all things vintage and, in her spare time, can be found digging for treasure at thrift stores and drinking coffee.

JEWELRY SUPPLIES AND BEADS

Beyond Beads
(semiprecious, glass, and vintage and new charms)
1251 Howard St., San Francisco, CA 94103
415-861-1685

Collage
(jewelry and craft supplies, beads, and ephemera)
3701 SE Division St., Portland, OR 97202
503-477-8804
www.collagepdx.com

Dava Bead & Trade
(vintage and new beads and findings)
2121 NE Broadway, Portland, OR 97232
503-288-3991
www.davabeadandtrade.com

Eloxite
(jewelry blanks, beads, and tools)
www.eloxite.com

Exclusive Buttons
(vintage buttons extraordinaire)
10252 San Pablo Ave., El Cerrito, CA 94530
510-524-5606

Fire Mountain Gems
(huge selection of glass, semiprecious, charms, metal, and more)
800-355-2137
www.firemountaingems.com

Michaels
(craft and jewelry supplies, silk flowers, paint, glass, and more)
800-MICHAELS
www.michaels.com

Ornamentea
(beads, ribbons, charms, and miscellany)
509 N. West St., Raleigh, NC 27603
919-834-6260
www.ornamentea.com

Rings & Things
(metal and findings of all kinds)
304 E. Second Ave., Spokane, WA 99202
800-366-2156
www.rings-things.com

Rio Grande
(semiprecious, metal, and tools)
7500 Bluewater Rd. NW,
Albuquerque, NM 87121
800-545-6566
www.riogrande.com

Toho Shoji N.Y.
(beads, chain, charms, and crystals)
990 Sixth Ave, New York, NY 10018
212-868-7465
www.tohoshoji-ny.com

FABRIC, LACE, AND TRIMS

Cotton+Steel
(fabric prints in beautiful designs)
2610 Columbia St., B
Torrance, CA 90503
855-355-7267
www.cottonandsteelfabrics.com

Fabric Depot
(huge fabric and notions selection)
700 SE 122nd Ave., Portland, OR 97233
800-392-3376
www.fabricdepot.com

JoAnn Fabric and Craft Stores®
(fabrics, notions, trims, and craft supplies)
www.joann.com
888-739-4120

M&J Trimming
(trims, ribbons, rhinestones, and more)
1008 Sixth Ave., New York, NY 10018
800-9MJ-TRIM
www.mjtrim.com

Pendleton Woolen Mill Store
(Pendleton wool fabrics and other sewing and craft supplies)
8500 SE McLoughlin Blvd.,
Portland, OR 97222
866-865-9285
www.thewoolenmillstore.blogspot.com

Renaissance Ribbons
(high-quality jacquard woven ribbons)
530-692-0842
www.renaissanceribbons.com

VINTAGE AND SECOND-HAND RESOURCES

Some of the best beads and jewelry supplies don't come from a craft store, but from a secondhand resource. Flea markets, consignment shops, thrift stores, and online retailers like Etsy and eBay often offer unique vintage and second-hand pieces that can be incorporated into your designs.

BOOKS

For lots more jewelry, accessories, and craft projects to make, please check out my other two jewelry books, *Bead Simple* and *Button It Up*.

A

Acrylic beads, 10

B

Barrettes
    Covered-Button Barrettes, 129
    Semiprecious Barrettes, 133
Beading, introduction to. *See* Getting started
Beading boards and trays, 14
Beading needles, 14
Beading resources, 184
Beading thread, invisible, 14
Beading wire, flexible, 14, 21
Beads, types and sizes of, 10–11, 12
    See also Crimp beads
Bead stitching, 31
Bead stringing
    crimp beads and clasps, 22
    finishing with bead tips, 20
    with flexible beading wire, 14, 21
    materials for, 14
    needle beading, 19–20
Bead tips, 20
Bookmark project, 173
Botanical décor, 162–64
Bracelet blanks and bangles, 7, 8
Bracelets, 141–60
    Angular Hexagons Bracelet, 154
    Beads & Briolette Charm Bracelet, 143
    Button Blossoms Bracelet, 147
    Button Box Bracelet, 156–57
    Cabochons & Rounds Bracelet, 150
    Charm Bangle Bracelet, 157
    Circle Cabochons Bracelet, 153
    Feathers Bracelet, 146–47
    Leaves on Chain Bracelet, 146
    Minimum Initials Charm Bracelet, 142
    Modern Traditional Charm Bracelet, 144
    Rainbow Button Bracelet, 156
    Semiprecious Charm Bracelets, 149
    Sparkle Bangle Bracelet, 159
    Sparkle Flowers Bracelet, 160
    Sparkle & Shine Bracelet, 159
    Wood Squares Bracelet, 152

Briolettes
    Beads & Briolette Charm Bracelet, 143
    Briolette Flower Clips, 123
    Circle & Briolette Drop Chain, 163–64
    wire wrapping techniques, 25–26
Brooches & barrettes, 120–39
    Bow Tie Brooch, 137
    Briolette Flower Clips, 123
    Butterfly Brooch, 136
    Covered-Button Barrettes, 129
    Filigree Flowers Hairpin, 139
    Floral Hair Clips, 139
    Ribbon Rosette Clip, 122
    Safety Pin Tassel Charm Brooch, 136
    Silk Flower Simplicity Clip, 121
    Solo Floral Hairpins, 139
    Square-Within-a-Square Brooch, 130
    Vintage Buttons Brooch, 129
    Into the Woods Fascinator, 127
Button designs
    barrettes, 129
    bracelets, 147, 156
    brooches, 129, 132, 136
    earrings, 60
    jars, 167
    pendants, 100
    picture frames, 174
Buttons, 11

C

Cabochon designs
    bracelets, 150, 153, 160
    brooches, 132, 137
    earrings, 60
    hairpins, 139
Chain/chains
    about, 9
    creating, 27
    mending, 33
Charm designs
    bracelets, 141–44
    brooches, 136
    earrings, 46
    handbags, 176
Clasps
    crimp clasps, 22
    making with wire, 28
    S-clasps, 29
    types of, 7

Clips
    Briolette Flower Clips, 123
    Floral Hair Clips, 139
    Rhinestone Clip, 176
    Silk Flower Simplicity Clip, 121
    types of, 7
Color
    combining, 15, 16
    as design principle, 150
Combs, hair, 124–27
Cord/cording, 9, 14
Corsage project, 178
Crimp beads, 7, 14, 22
Crimp clasps, 22
Cross-stitch pattern, 32

D

Dangles, basic, 25
Delica beads, 10
Design principles
    botanicals, 66
    color, color, color, 150
    elongated *vs.* compact, 103
    explained, 17
    graphic and linear, 174
    mixing high and low materials, 132
    mixing metals, 142
    negative space, 154
    somewhere for the eye to land, 97
    vintage meets modern, 13
Designs
    color combinations in, 15, 16
    ideas for, 16
Double-looped bead connectors, 25
Double-wrapped loops, 26

E

Earrings, 36–60
    Dual Circles Earrings, 50
    Earth Tone Tassel Earrings, 39
    Family Birthstone Earrings, 54
    Filigree Circles Earrings, 60
    Filigree Leaves Earrings, 47
    Floral Charm Drop Earrings, 46
    Floral Post Earrings, 60
    Geometric earrings, 48–51
    Hanging Triangles Earrings, 49

Little Trio Earrings, 53
Loop-d-Loop Earrings, 42–43
Northern Lights Earrings, 58
Orange Crush Earrings, 38
Pearl Loops Earrings, 51
Pearls & Petals Earrings, 46–47
Pearls & Rings Earrings, 57
Pretty Curve Earrings, 53
Sparkle Tassel Earrings, 44
Sunset Earrings, 40
Treasure Jar Earrings, 56
Vintage Earrings, 60
Vintage Tinsel Earrings, 43
Earring wires, 7, 28
Embellished hair combs, 124–27
Embellishments, 162–81
    Bead & Button Jars, 167
    Beaded Vase Necklace, 164
    Charming Corsages, 178
    Circle & Briolette Drop Chain, 163–64
    Embellished Label Jars, 166–67
    Geometric Magnets, 173
    Lovebirds Handbag Charm, 176
    Quick Bookmark, 173
    Rhinestone Clip, 176
    Sequin Flowers Handbag, 181
    Sparkle Flower Jars, 166
    Sparkle Flowers Handbag, 179
    Star Shadow Box Ornament, 171
    Tassels on Chain, 163
    Three Rings Handbag, 180
    Tiny Tree Terrarium, 170
    Trio of Buttons Picture Frame, 174
    Vintage Stamp Ornaments, 169
Embellishments, types of, 10–11
Ephemera and mixed media, 12–13
Etsy and eBay, 13
Eyepins, 7, 28

F
Fabrics and threads, 12, 14
Family pendants, 94–97
Fascinator project, 127
Favorite designs. *See* My favorite designs
Findings, types of, 6–7, 7, 8
Flexible beading wire, 14, 21
Floral designs
    bracelets, 160

clips, 121, 123
earrings, 46, 60
hairpins, 139
handbags, 179, 181
jars, 166
necklaces, 84, 90, 92–93
pendants, 108, 117

G
Geometric designs
    bracelets, 151–54
    earrings, 48–51
    magnets, 173
    necklaces, 63
Getting started, 5–17
    beads, 10–11
    color combinations, 15, 16
    cords, wires, and threads, 14
    design basics, 16, 17
    findings, 6–7
    mixed media and ephemera, 12–13
    needles, 14
    stringing, 14
    tools, 5–6
    vintage treasures, 13
    wire, 8–9
Gifts, 172–74
Glass beads, 10
Glues/gluing, 5–6, 33

H
Hair clips and hairpins, 129, 133, 138–39
Hair combs, embellished, 124–27
Handbag projects, 176, 179, 180, 181
Headpins, 7
Holiday ornaments, 168–71
Holiday party necklaces, 72–76
Hooks, forming, 28

J
Jar and vase projects, ceramic, 162–64
Jar projects, glass, 165–67
Jewelry and bead resources, 184
Jewelry pliers, 5, *6*
Jewelry repair, 33
Jump rings, 6, *7,* 27, 33

K
Knotting
    between beads, 30
    reknotting beads, 33

L
Lace and trims, 12–13
    See also Ribbons
Loops, forming, 23–24, 26
Lucite beads, 10

M
Magnet project, 173
Materials for beading, 6–13
Metal beads, 10
Mixed media and ephemera, 12–13
My favorite designs
    bracelets, 155–57
    earrings, 55–58
    embellishments, 175–77
    necklaces, 85–88

N
Nature-inspired projects
    brooches & barrettes, 120–23
    earrings, 45–47
    necklaces, 64–68
    pendants, 105–8
Necklaces, 62–92
    Amber Floral Necklace, 90
    Beaded Vase Necklace, 164
    Black & Gold Floral Necklace, 92–93
    Blue Floral Necklace, 92
    Deco Sparkle Necklace, 80
    Floral Appliqué Statement Necklace, 84
    Forest Park Necklace, 66–67
    Geometric Trio Necklace, 63
    Gold & Coral Necklace, 87
    Jade & Adenturine Links Necklace, 70–71
    Ladder of Pearls Necklace, 88
    Midcentury Color Whirl Necklace, 78–79
    Midcentury Turquoise Drops Necklace, 71
    Modern Lucite Necklace, 81
    Northern Lights Necklace, 68
    Octopus Necklace, 83
    Ovals & Circles Necklace, 63
    Sea Glass Necklace, 66
    Sunset Necklace, 75–76

R

epairing jewelry, 33
hinestones, 11
bbons
    in clips, 122
    as embellishments, 12–13
    narrow, 14
    in pendants, 106, 111
gs, 6, *7*
nning stitch, 30

clasps, 29
ed beads, 10
miprecious beads
    bracelets, 148–50
    brooches & barrettes, 131–34
    earrings, 52–54
    necklaces, 69–71
    pendants, 101–4
    using, 10
quins, 11
arkle designs
    bracelets, 159, 160
    earrings, 44
    handbags, 179
    jars, 166
    necklaces, 73–74, 80
    pendants, 113
atement necklaces, 82–84
tching techniques, 30–32
inging beads. *See* Bead stringing

chniques, 18–33
    bead stringing, 19–22
    jewelry repair, 33
    knotting and reknotting, 30, 33
    stitching, 30–32
    wirework, 23–29
eads, 9, 12, 14
red necklaces, 77–81
ols, 5–6
e terrarium project, 170
ns and lace, 12–13
    See also Ribbons

V

Vase and jar projects, 162–64
Vintage gone modern projects
    bracelets, 158–60
    brooches & barrettes, 138–39
    earrings, 59–60
    embellishments, 178–81
    necklaces, 89–92
    pendants, 116–18
Vintage pieces, using, 13

W

Wire
    and findings, 6–7, 8
    flexible beading wire, 14, 21
    gauges of, 9
    types of, 8–9
Wire cutters, 5, 6
Wirework, 23–29
    basic dangle, 25
    basic earring wires, 28
    briolette wrapping, 25–26
    clasps, 28, 29
    double-looped bead connector, 25
    double-wrapped loop, 26
    eyepins, 28
    hooks, 28
    jump rings, 27
    plain loops, 23
    wrapped loops, 24
Wood beads, 10
Wrapped loops, 24

Discover the world of *Threads*.

Read *Threads* Magazine:

Your subscription includes six issues of *Threads* plus FREE tablet editions. Every issue is packed with up-to-the-minute fashions, useful techniques, and expert garment-sewing advice – all designed to help improve your skills and express your creativity.

Subscribe today at:
ThreadsMagazine.com/4Sub

Shop our *Threads* Online Store:

It's your destination for premium resources from the editors of America's best-loved sewing magazine, designers, and sewing instructors: how-to and design books, videos, and more.

Visit today at:
ThreadsMagazine.com/4More

Become a Threads Insider:

Join now and enjoy exclusive online benefits, including: instant videos, favorite articles, digital issues, pattern database, and more.

Discover more information online:
ThreadsMagazine.com/4Join

Get our FREE *Threads* e-Newsletter:

Keep up with what's current – the latest styles, patterns, and fabrics, plus free tips and advice from our *Threads* editors.

Sign up, it's free:
ThreadsMagazine.com/4Newsletter